BUT GOD

A Story of God using Ordinary People in Extraordinary Ways in the World's Most Difficult Places

Stan Buckley (signature)

STAN BUCKLEY

But God
404 Fontaine pl
Suite 104
Ridgeland MS 39157

ISBN: 978-1-6847-1350-9 (sc)
ISBN: 978-1-6847-1349-3 (e)

Because of the dynamic nature of the Internet, any web addresses or links contained in this book may have changed since publication and may no longer be valid. The views expressed in this work are solely those of the author and do not necessarily reflect the views of the publisher, and the publisher hereby disclaims any responsibility for them.

Scripture taken from the Holy Bible, NEW INTERNATIONAL VERSION®. Copyright © 1973, 1978, 1984, 2011 by Biblica, Inc. All rights reserved worldwide. Used by permission. NEW INTERNATIONAL VERSION® and NIV® are registered trademarks of Biblica, Inc. Use of either trademark for the offering of goods or services requires the prior written consent of Biblica US, Inc.

Any people depicted in stock imagery provided by Getty Images are models, and such images are being used for illustrative purposes only. Certain stock imagery © Getty Images.

Lulu Publishing Services rev. date: 11/12/2019

CONTENTS

To Adam, Neal, and Anna

CHAPTER 1

In The Beginning

There I was, standing in a tent city in a remote location in Haiti seven months after the January 2010 earthquake. But it was no ordinary tent city, if there is such a thing. It was a tent city for amputees.

My journey to Haiti had started a few weeks earlier when a guy named Tim Dortch came to my office. My office was located at First Baptist Church, Jackson, Mississippi where I was serving as the Senior Pastor. I wasn't sure how Tim had gotten an appointment to see me. I had no desire to see him because I knew what he wanted. He wanted to discuss Haiti. I wasn't opposed to Haiti. I had no ill will towards that impoverished country. I just wasn't interested. After all, at a church with over 5,000 members, multiple campuses, a $9 million budget, 30 ministerial staff, and almost 200 full-time and part-time employees, I had plenty to do. I didn't need someone else's project.

Tim sat on the couch in my office, opened his laptop, and began to share the work he was doing in Haiti. Tim had a compound next door to Haiti in the Dominican Republic ("DR") where he had worked for over 10 years. After the earthquake struck in Haiti, the border between the two countries was opened, and relief supplies flowed freely. Tim crossed the border and began offering whatever assistance he could.

As he talked, Tim showed me photos of the tent cities that had sprung up in Haiti.

After he shared all he wanted to share, I said a little prayer for him, patted him on the back, and ushered him out the door. Finally, I was rid of this guy, and I could get back to all the important work that was on my schedule. But there was a problem. I couldn't get the photos of those tent cities out of my mind. Thousands and thousands of people, tens of thousands of people, were living in filth and squalor and hopelessness. I prayed, "Lord, I live in a nice house in Madison, Mississippi. Why do these people have to live in tents? It shouldn't be this way."

For several days I thought about all those people living in all those tents. Finally, I decided I would go. I would check it out and see if there was any way we could help. I had no idea what that help might look like but decided to go anyway.

While having lunch with landscape architect Mark Rich, I mentioned that I was about to travel to Haiti to get a first-hand look at the damage from the earthquake. He said, "Are you serious? I think I'm supposed to go to Haiti." And he decided to go with me. A few days later, I ran into Mallory Rosamond in the break room of our church. I asked her to come to my office so we could talk. Mallory was the 26 year-old leader of Women's Ministries at First Baptist Jackson. She led hundreds of ladies in countless mission activities.

Mallory showed up in my office about ten minutes later, and I told her Mark and I were going to Haiti and asked if she wanted to go with us. She said, "You won't believe this but last week I was across the street at the Mississippi Baptist Convention headquarters meeting with the State Director of our women's work. She was trying to get me to go to Africa. Finally, I told her I appreciated her efforts in Africa, but I thought I was supposed to go to Haiti. And here I am talking to you about going to Haiti!"

I said, "Mallory, I have two questions. Do you have a

passport, and can you go to Haiti on Monday?" She said yes to both, and off we went!

It was August 23, 2010 when Mark, Mallory, Tim, and I flew into Santo Domingo, the capital of the DR. Haiti and the DR share an island called Hispaniola. Haiti sits on the west side of the island and the DR on the east. The island is just east of Cuba, which is only 90 miles from the coast of Florida.

We spent the first night of our trip at Tim's compound located about an hour from the Haitian border. The next day we crossed into Haiti, and that's when I came to my first tent city. It was in a rural setting not far from the border. As we exited our van, I was shocked to see so many people with missing limbs -- arms and legs, hands and feet, all amputated as a result of the earthquake. The missing limbs, coupled with the overwhelming poverty, was difficult to process, so I walked away from our group to get my thoughts together. While doing so, I found myself walking down a pathway surrounded by tents. As I walked, I looked and saw a young Haitian man about 19 or 20 years old walking towards me. I soon learned his name was Thoman, and he spoke great English.

Thomas appeared to have all his limbs intact, so I asked him how he ended up in this particular tent city. He said, "During the earthquake, my dad was killed, my home was destroyed, my school was destroyed, and my mom became an amputee. That's how we ended up here." I then asked him what it was like living in that tent city. After all, by that time he had been there over seven months. Thomas didn't complain, he just answered my question. He said, "It's not good here. The water is not good, and the food is not good."

I said, "How do you survive each day, mentally and emotionally?"

Thomas didn't know who I was or what I did for a living, but he said, "There's a book in the Bible called Ecclesiastes. In that book it says there is a time for everything. A time to laugh and a time to cry. Sometimes we laugh, and sometimes we cry."

Then I asked Thomas what is probably the dumbest question any human has ever asked another. I said, "Thomas, if it were possible for you and your mom and your friends to move out of this tent city and into a community where there was clean water, heathy food, decent housing, a school, and jobs, would you be interested in moving from here into that kind of place?"

He must have thought, "What kind of question is that? Is this guy a nut?" But I will never forget the reply of Thomas. He said, "Of course we would be interested, but that's impossible!"

Now, God has yet to speak to me audibly. I can't wait for that day, but it hasn't happened yet. Nonetheless, as soon as Thomas said those words, "that's impossible," the Spirit of God spoke two words to my spirit: But God. It was as clear and direct as anything I have ever heard. But God. And suddenly my mind began to race through the Scriptures as I recalled all the times God has shown up in impossible situations. After all, that's when He does His best work. I thought about the Israelites at the Red Sea. I thought about the lions' den and the fiery furnace.

Then my mind jumped to the New Testament, and I thought about the most impossible situation any of us has ever faced. Ephesians 2 tells us we were dead in our trespasses and sins. Dead. Just dead people walking. No spiritual life. No hope, no future, and nothing we could do about it. Dead. But that's not the end of the story. It goes on to say, "But . . . God, who is rich in mercy, made us alive with Christ Jesus!"

Wow! What a God! What hope! What promise! I thought about all those things while Thomas was standing two feet in front of me. And then . . . I left. It was time to go. I got into the van with Mark, Mallory, and Tim, and we drove to Port-au-Prince. There, I saw endless rubble blocking streets and alleys. There, I saw trash everywhere. There, I went to the 50,000 person tent city run by the actor Sean Penn. There, I saw hopelessness and despair as I had never seen before.

We spent the night in Petionville, just south of Port-au-Prince, and then it was time to go. We traveled back across the border, spent the night in a hotel in Santo Domingo, and flew home the next day. Over the next few days, I prayed, "God, what am I supposed to do now? You've shown me overwhelming needs. You've shown me people who are hurting and suffering. You've shown me utter and complete poverty. What am I supposed to do now?"

WHAT NOW?

As I prayed and talked with others about what we could do in Haiti, God began to give us a vision for a sustainable community for people still living in tents. This community would consist of: 40 houses, water wells, a medical-dental complex, a church, a school, agriculture plots, and a soccer field. Over time, the community would also include an orphanage and economic development - job training and job creation.

The key for us was the word sustainability. We wanted to build something that would last and that, eventually, would not be dependent on us. In the past, I had participated in what I call "parachute missions." You drop in somewhere for a week, do some nice things, then leave. You feel good about what you did, but when you leave so does the work. It doesn't last. I didn't want to be part of those kinds of efforts anymore. If we were going to do something in Haiti, it would have to be an ongoing project that would last for many years and would empower the people of Haiti to support themselves. We were not interested in handouts. Handouts don't work in America, and they don't work in Haiti. We wanted to give a hand-up. We wanted to provide opportunities for Haitians, opportunities to work and to provide for their own families, opportunities for jobs that give dignity, hope, and a future. In short, a sustainable community.

This all sounded great, but there was one big problem. The cost to build a community from scratch on an island in the

Caribbean would likely be substantial, and I didn't have a dime to do it. Nothing. Not one penny. But I would soon be reminded that God owns the cattle on a thousand hills.

For over a month we planned and prayed and thought and developed. We built a prototype of a house we thought we could make in the States, ship to Haiti, and then quickly assemble. We would learn later that complications related to shipping would prohibit us from building houses in this way, but at the time we thought that was the way to go.

On Sunday, October 17, 2010, the people of First Baptist Jackson entered the sanctuary to find a large, white house sitting on the platform. It was 18 feet long, 12 feet wide, and 15 feet tall. This was the house we thought we would build and ship to Haiti. That day, I shared the vision God had given us for a sustainable community in Haiti. I talked about the trip Mark, Mallory, and I had made to Haiti six weeks earlier. I showed photos of the trip. I gave the Biblical rationale for why we would do this.

Then I shared the way we could finance the construction of this sustainable community. I announced that the following March we would have a special Ingathering Sunday in which we would take an offering for this work. I shared with them the cost of a house (which at the time we thought would cost $3,000) and told them my family was going to give enough to build one house. I told them they could do the same, or they could give enough for half a house, or a door, or a window, or whatever God was leading them to give.

The next Sunday we were set to broadcast the worship service from the previous week that included the vision of the sustainable community in Haiti. For years, First Baptist Jackson has had a television broadcast across much of the state of Mississippi and a national broadcast on Directv. The services have a one week delay so that each Sunday we broadcast the previous week's service.

I decided to film a short segment that would play at the

end of the broadcast. In this segment, I told the television audience that we had been broadcasting our services since 1956 and had never asked for a dime for the services, and we never would. The services are a gift from the church to the community. However, they had heard what we were doing in Haiti, and if they wanted to contribute to that work they could certainly do so. I said, "We have learned that most people know about the earthquake in Haiti, and most people want to help. They simply don't know who they can trust with their money." I then said, "You know you can trust us. You watch us every week. We have been here for 173 years, and we're not going anywhere. We're directly across the street from the state capitol as well as the Mississippi Baptist Convention. We have more financial controls in place than any other organization I know. We will use your gift exactly as we say." And then I was able to give them one more piece of information. I said, "One hundred percent of your gift will go towards the building of this community in Haiti. Our church will handle the administrative costs."

And with that, we had been obedient. We had shared the vision. We had explained the process. Then we waited.

I WAS THINKING . . .

I saw it. Again. The desperately poor. Last week in Haiti I saw that family of 8 that lives in . . . well, I don't know what you call it. It's about 12 feet by 10 feet. Has a piece of plastic for a roof. Some thatch on the sides. Dirt for a floor. And that's where they sleep. In the dirt.

Food? I asked her what they ate the previous night. Corn. What would they eat that night? Maybe some rice. And a few beans. The night after that? Didn't ask.

They're poor. Not lazy. Not apathetic. Not bad. Poor. Uneducated. Can't read and can't write. Surrounded by exactly zero opportunities to better themselves. Desperately poor.

Wish I could have been there. That day when Peter, James, and John met with Paul and Barnabas. Five giants of the faith together in one room. Men who would be used by God to change the world. What would they discuss? What great and deep and holy topic would be the center of their talks? What complicated doctrine would occupy their precious time? What aspect of complex theology would be the focus of their attention?

One thing. Only one thing Peter, James, and John asked of Paul and Barnabas in Galatians 2:10. One thing. In all the world of Christianity, they asked one thing: Remember the poor. That's what they wanted their new Christian friends to do. Remember the poor.

Paul? Loved it. Said that was the very thing he was eager to do. The VERY thing.

What do I talk about, you ask, when I get together with Christian friends to discuss matters of faith? Please don't ask. Seems the things I end up talking about have nothing to do with the one thing the great heroes of the faith talked about. Sometimes I wonder what they would think if they heard some of our conversations today. Would they shake their heads? Would they stare in disbelief? Would their faces grow red until the volatile Peter exploded in anger shouting at us, "What are you talking about!?! People are hungry and dying and helpless! People have no hope! They do not know God! They are sick and poor and uneducated! And you people have everything. EVERYTHING! And you spend exactly zero time talking about how to use your blessings to bless them! YOU. DON'T. GET IT!"

May God grant us wisdom in His church to forsake pointless discussions of things that do not matter. May he forgive us for wasting precious time and resources on things that will make no difference in anyone's life. May he help us to do the one thing his faithful servants discussed so long ago: remember the poor.

CHAPTER 2

But God Provisions

After five months of waiting, March 6, 2011 finally arrived. That was the day of the special Ingathering Offering for the community in Haiti. The plan that day was for me to preach a regular sermon, and then we would take up the special offering. After the second morning service, the Counting Committee would stay at the church and count the offering. Then, we would all come back for an evening service in which we would announce the total and have a great celebration.

Normally, you have some idea of what an offering will be. You've taken similar offerings and year-to-year they are fairly close. But this was different. This was like no other offering we had taken. We had no idea what the total would be.

After preaching that morning, I went home for lunch. The plan was for our Executive Pastor, Bob Gladney, to call me as soon as he received the total from the Counting Committee. At 1:00, no Bob. At 2:00, no Bob. At 3:00 and 4:00, still no call from Bob. I was getting nervous. I began to think the worst. "Nobody gave. This will be embarrassing. Maybe one little boy gave $8 and that's all. How will I announce the pitiful total?" At 5:00 Bob still had not called, but it was time for me to drive downtown for the evening service. As I drove out of my neighborhood, I called Bob. "What's going on? Why haven't you called?"

Bob asked, "Are you sitting down?"

I said, "Yes, I'm driving."

He said, "You might want to pull over. The total so far, including all that has been given since you shared the vision last October, is right at $500,000." And I thought two words: But God.

Through His people, God had provided half a million dollars for this work. $500,000 had been given, not merely pledged. Five months earlier we had exactly zero dollars for this work. Nothing. Nada. Zip. Zilch. And there we were, five months later, and God was showing Himself in a real, powerful, and tangible way. But God, indeed!

All kinds of people gave to what we called, "The Haiti Project." There was Allen. Allen the Cub Scout. Allen was seven years old in March of 2011, and he lived with his family in one of the suburbs outside of Jackson, Mississippi. In the summer of 2010, Allen spent a week in Texas with his grandmother. During that week, he went to Vacation Bible School at his grandmother's church. One day he came home from Bible School and asked his grandmother, "Do you know the name of the King of Haiti?"

She said, "No I don't, but why do you ask?" Allen told her that at Bible School that day they had been told about the horrible earthquake in Haiti and he wanted to send some money to the King of Haiti so he could help his people. Allen's grandmother smiled as she thought about this beautiful gesture on the part of Allen.

Months later, Allen's grandmother was talking on the phone to her own mother, Allen's great-grandmother, who was living in a retirement home in a different part of Texas. The grandmother told her mom what Allen had said about the King of Haiti. The great-grandmother said, "He should send some money to my TV church. They're helping out in Haiti." Her TV church was our church, First Baptist Jackson. She had seen the broadcast when I shared the vision of the sustainable community.

So, Allen went to work. He began raising money through

his Cub Scout troop. He began asking his friends and family members to give. In a myriad of ways, Allen collected money for the people of Haiti. And then, on March 13, 2011, Allen came to our services at First Baptist Jackson. We brought him onto the platform. I introduced him to the congregation, and Allen presented us with a check for $3,400 to go towards the cost of a house in Haiti! A seven year-old Cub Scout raised over three thousand dollars! What an incredible little boy. I shall never forget the heart and love of Allen the Cub Scout.

I was especially blessed when my 11th grade son, Adam, decided he wanted to save his allowance, Christmas gifts, and paychecks to go towards a house. He managed to save hundreds of dollars and then his grandmother made up the difference so that at our Ingathering Sunday in March 2011 he was able to give the cost of an entire house in Haiti. I was so proud!

One day after we had shared the vision for the new sustainable community, a wonderful Christian man and his wife came to my office. They said they were thrilled with the work we were proposing in Haiti. They were faithful members of the church but not high profile members. They were not well known throughout the congregation. They held no specific positions in the church. They were simply godly, faithful members.

They walked into my office that day and informed me they had originally thought they would give a gift to build five houses. But the more they thought about it, they decided to double the amount and give enough money to build ten houses. Ten! By themselves! But God!

We began receiving gifts from around the country. A couple from southern California began giving monthly. One day I called to thank them, and during the conversation I asked how they had heard about the project and what caused them to want to get involved.

They said they had watched the national broadcast on Directv back when I shared the vision of the sustainable community. As I shared, they looked at one another and knew this was something in which they should participate. They said they had been praying God would give them a focus for their energies and resources, and when they saw this project on the broadcast, they knew this was it. This couple has given faithfully for eight years and has played a huge role in repairing the terrible road that leads to our place in Haiti, providing a bus for our teams, and helping build our new medical-dental complex in the mountains. They are dear friends who, as the Apostle Paul would say, are partners in the gospel.

Another person who was a great blessing in our work in Haiti was a 92 year-old lady from Bessemer, Alabama named Lorine Adkins. Like others, she watched our service from First Baptist Jackson on Directv every week and began giving monthly to the work in Haiti. She told me numerous times she knew God was in this work. She prayed for us daily and was one of the greatest encouragers I have ever known. Every month she sent $45.

Once I was driving through Birmingham and had some extra time. I looked up Ms. Lorine's address and drove to Bessemer. I found her house, parked in front, and walked to the front door. I knocked on the door, and Ms. Lorine answered. She immediately recognized me from watching First Baptist Jackson all those years. She invited me in. We had a wonderful visit, and I was able to thank her personally for all her support and encouragement. But God!

All of these examples are just a few of the many ways God provided in the early days of our work to build a sustainable community in Haiti. God has made a way when there seemed to be no way. He has provided in the face of overwhelming odds, and we stand amazed at His grace, His goodness, and His provisions.

I WAS THINKING . . .

Why not? Why not you? Oh, I know. You're not smart enough, or pretty enough, or wealthy enough. You don't have the right degree or the right friends or the right . . . something. And that past. Oh, that past. If people only knew. No, it can't be you.

But if you had all these things you could be the one. You could get it done. And you'd be glad to. If you had all these things and if you were all these things, you could feed the hungry, befriend the lonely, or comfort the hurting. You could love the unlovely and forgive the guilty. You could share His love and spread His word and teach His plan. But you don't have all these things. You're not all these things. So God can't use you. He would probably like to, but He just can't.

After all, only the really smart people and the really beautiful people and the really rich people can feed the hungry and comfort the hurting and visit the imprisoned. Only the perfect people can take care of the widows and the orphans. Only the flawless people can share His love and encourage the downtrodden and embrace the suffering.

Well, except for Abraham. And Moses. And Rahab and David and Peter and Timothy and Paul. They were liars and killers and prostitutes and adulterers and traitors and nobodies and murderers.

And except for Rick and Tony and John and Mallory and Cathy and Dale and Diana. And, of course, Sam and Melanie and Wayne and Jill and June and James. All not-so-famous friends of mine who are doing amazing things in the name of our amazing God. Somewhere along the way they stopped making excuses and decided to be obedient. No matter the cost. No matter the obstacles. No matter their insecurities or inabilities. They just said yes to God.

You see, it really wasn't about them. It wasn't about their skills or their looks or their bank accounts. It was about Him. It was about His plan and His strength and His wisdom.

So we ask. Why not? Why not you?

CHAPTER 3

But God Events

Following the Ingathering Sunday of March, 2011, many But God stories began to occur. In April of that year, I was speaking at Jackson State University when Barbara Gladney called. Barbara is the wife of Bob, who was the Executive Pastor of First Baptist Jackson. Barbara played a pivotal role in the development of our work in Haiti. After she heard me share the vision with the church in October, 2010, she told Bob on the way home from church she was going to volunteer to help me with the project. She said there was no way I could lead such a large church and, at the same time, tend to the details of building a sustainable community in an impoverished Caribbean island. She was right. The work in Haiti quickly became much bigger and more complex than I had imagined. Barbara is a detail person. She knows what happened, when it happened, and who made it happen. She knows what is supposed to happen next, who is supposed to be involved, how much it will cost, and how long it should take. Without Barbara, we could not have progressed so rapidly as we did in the early days of our work.

For months, people had been saying the same thing to me. They would say, "I know what you're going to do. You're going to send medical and dental teams down to Haiti to work in the clinic. But you can't send a team every week of the year.

What's going to happen to the clinic when you don't have a team there? Will it just sit there being idle?" I gave the same answer to everyone who asked me that question. I told them I was believing by faith that God was going to provide a doctor or nurse who would commit to serving several years in Haiti." But we never advertised this idea. We never put it in the bulletin or on the screens or in a mass email. We just believed.

On that day in April of 2011 when I was at Jackson State, Barbara asked if I would like to hear some good news. I said, "By all means, give me some good news."

She said, "You won't believe this, but . . ." I love when a sentence starts that way! She said, "you won't believe this, but I just got off the phone with a guy who said, 'You don't know me, but my name is Tony West. I am an RN, and I have a master's degree in Health Care Administration. For years I have been running multiple Hospice Centers around the state. A year ago, shortly after the earthquake, I went to Haiti three times to work in the cholera clinics of Samaritan's Purse. Now, a year later, I believe God is calling me to move myself and my family to Haiti to operate a medical clinic on a full-time basis. We're not sure where or how, but we hear you guys may be doing something.'"

I said, "Barbara, Tony may not know where or how, but you and God and I do!"

Barbara and Tony decided to meet the following week for lunch to talk further. As they sat down to talk, Tony told Barbara about a dream he had that week. He said, "In my dream, there was a community in Haiti that had a medical-dental clinic, houses around it, a soccer field, water wells, and agriculture plots." Barbara sat back and smiled. As Tony finished, Barbara reached into her bag and pulled out a diagram of the community we were about to begin building.

She asked, "Did the community in your dream look like this?"
Tony said, "That's it! That's exactly what I saw in my dream!"
And I said, "But God!"
In the fall of 2012, Tony West and his wife, Mickie, moved

to Haiti as our full-time missionaries. Tony left a successful career as an administrator at a Hospice organization that had facilities around the state of Mississippi. Mickie was a high school English teacher as well an adjunct English professor at Mississippi College. Their oldest son, Jonathan, was in college at the time. He stayed in Mississippi to finish his degree. Their youngest son, Jacob, was a junior in high school and moved to Haiti with his parents. He was an outstanding soccer player, and the plan was for him to play with one of the Haitian national teams. That plan did work out and, after a number of months, Mickie moved back to the States for Jacob to play with his high school soccer team and finish school. For a year and a half, Mickie and Jacob would spend all holidays as well as the summer before Jacob's senior year in Haiti. Then after Jacob graduated, Mickie returned to Haiti full-time.

Tony gives administrative leadership to the clinic as well as leadership to everything we do in Galette Chambon. Amazingly, he earned his nurse practitioner's degree from Samford University while serving in Haiti. This required numerous trips to Birmingham to Samford's campus as well as countless clinic hours. But, Tony persevered and earned his degree. Just amazing!

Mickie has two primary responsibilities in Haiti. First, she gives leadership to our school sponsorship program and the three schools in which we operate. Mickie formed a new "school district" for these three schools. In addition, she single-handedly started the sponsorship program and got over 400 children sponsored. Also, Mickie coordinates the activities of the mission teams and makes sure everything is ready when they arrive at the Hope Center.

Tony and Mickie have done remarkable work over the last seven years in Haiti. Living in Haiti is not easy. In fact, it's very hard. The roads are awful and beat you to death. The traffic in Port-au-Prince is maddening. Everything breaks. Constantly. The vehicles break, the generators break, the appliances break. The wells break, the water pumps break, the medical equipment breaks. There is always something in need of repair.

Then, there are the language difficulties and the cultural challenges. There are misunderstandings with the locals. There is sometimes confusion and lack of trust. There are issues with nothing starting on time and locals being late for everything. There are constant problems. But Tony and Mickie have persevered. They have stayed the course. They are still there. Without their willingness to stay and fight, we would not be where we are today in Haiti.

At the end of May 2011, we began construction of the sustainable community in Haiti. Instead of building houses first, we began building The Hope Center. The Hope Center has numerous buildings inside a round wall: (1) a medical clinic, (2) a dental clinic, (3) four dorms for visiting American teams, complete with air conditioning units, (4) a building with kitchen/bathrooms/showers, (5) a three bedroom house for our American Medical Director missionary and his family, (6) a two bedroom house for another American missionary, and (7) a small room for my regular visits.

The reason we built The Hope Center with the medical-dental clinic prior to building the houses is because the locals requested us to do so. When I asked why, one Haitian said to me, "If my wife or child is sick, I cannot afford to take them to Port-au-Prince to see a doctor. If I could afford to take them to Port-au-Prince, I could not afford to pay the doctor. And if I could afford to take them to Port-au-Prince, and if I could afford pay the doctor, I could not afford the medicine. So please build the medical clinic first."

And we said, "Yes, we will build the medical-dental clinic first."

After the Hope Center was completed, we needed a large generator to supply power to all five buildings. One day a gentleman took his daughter to visit a pediatric dentist named Lee Cope who serves on the Board of But God Ministries. As

Dr. Cope began to examine the girl, the father asked Dr. Cope how he was doing. Dr. Cope explained that he had become involved in work in Haiti and we were looking to acquire a generator to supply the Hope Center with electricity. The man said that his company makes generators and asked Dr. Cope to send the specs for the generators to his engineers. Later that evening, Dr. Cope did so.

A couple of weeks later the man brought his daughter back to Dr. Cope's office for a follow-up visit. The man said to Dr. Cope, "Before we get started with the dental work, I want to talk about the generator for Haiti. We are going to do two generators, and one of them is powerful enough to run your entire office here in the States."

Dr. Cope asked, "What do you mean you are going to 'do' two generators?"

The man said, "We are going to build and donate two generators."

Dr. Cope asked him, "How much would these generators cost if you were selling them?"

The man said, "$25,000 each." Dr. Cope called me with the news, and I thought two words: But God!

While it was great news to receive the donated generators, we had a problem. Each generator weighs 1,600 pounds, a little too big to fit into our checked bags on the plane to Haiti. We were going to have to ship them to Haiti in a container. Our problem was getting them from Jackson, MS. to a port near Ft. Lauderdale, Florida.

A couple of months before, a member of First Baptist Jackson called me and asked if I would visit her 90 year-old dad in a nursing home. Even though he was not a member of the church, I told her I would be glad to go. I went, and we had a great visit. A few weeks later he died. The lady called and asked if I would conduct the funeral service. I told her I would be happy to and asked if she had anyone to sing. She said she did not, so I got the Minister of Music at First Baptist Jackson,

Lavon Gray, to sing at the service. It was a graveside service on a beautiful, sun-drenched day. Lavon did a great job singing a cappella, and I preached a simple message for a 90 year-old Christian.

The next Sunday, Barbara Gladney spoke in the Sunday School class of the lady whose father had died. Barbara gave them an update about the progress in Haiti. Afterwards, the lady told Barbara to let her know if we needed any help such as shipping. Barbara thanked her but did not think much about it until we realized we needed to ship the generators to Ft. Lauderdale. She told me what the lady said, and I called the lady to see if she had any information about shipping. She said she did. She said her son was the President and CEO of a large trucking company located in Jackson. She gave me her son's number and told me to call him.

I called the son and explained to him our situation. He said he would be glad to help. I said, "But you don't understand. You would have to pick up these large generators in Jackson and then drive to Pensacola and pick up an entire truckload of items that need to be shipped to Haiti along with the generators."

He said, "We'll pick up the generators in Jackson, drive to Pensacola, pick up those items, and then haul them all to Ft. Lauderdale."

I said, "How much will that cost?"

He said, "I told you, we'll pick up the generators in Jackson, drive to Pensacola, pick up those items, and then haul them all to Ft. Lauderdale. We haul goods in all 48 contiguous states. It won't cost you anything." And I thought, But God!

In the beginning, there was no plan for an orphanage to be associated with But God Ministries. Then, two churches in Pensacola contacted me about holding a medical clinic at the Hope Center and sending teams on mission trips. The churches were First Baptist Church Pensacola, FL and Hillcrest Baptist Church in Pensacola. These two churches do missions together. What a concept! Churches working together for the glory of God and the benefit of others. Why haven't more churches figured this out?!?

I agreed to travel to Pensacola and speak at Hillcrest Wednesday night, December 14, 2011, and share about the work in which we were engaged. Before the meeting that night, I met three people from these churches for lunch. As we talked, they kept mentioning an orphanage they had worked with south of Port-au-Prince. Several times they mentioned this orphanage and how the orphanage needed to move out of the city into a more rural area. Finally, I said, "Let's just stop this conversation. I want you to know that I don't want to build an orphanage. I don't want to raise money for an orphanage. I don't want to continuously support an orphanage." There was an awkward silence. Then I said, "But I would love to partner with someone who wants to do these things." Immediately, there was a sense of relief and then excitement on the faces of these men. We talked further and they agreed to build and then fund an orphanage that would be a part of But God Ministries. In March 2013 the orphanage buildings were completed, and children began moving in shortly thereafter.

As the orphanage was being built, I shared some concerns with the U.S. leaders of the orphanage. All of the leadership lives in Pensacola and, as previously noted, are members of two churches there. I told them my concern was that one day their current pastors would move to other churches, and they would get new pastors. Those new pastors might be far more interested in Honduras than Haiti. What that usually means is that the church gets involved in Honduras. Then, I would be left with an orphanage that I had not envisioned in the first place. I told them that the only way to avoid this problem would be for them to form a separate 501(c)(3) non-profit organization to support the orphanage.

They agreed and formed the Children of Christ Home non-profit organization to fund and operate the orphanage. Al Stubblefield is the President of the Children of Christ Home

Board of Directors. Al retired from his role as the President of Baptist Health Systems in Pensacola. Al is one of the most reasonable, wise, solid, easy-to-work-with people I have ever known. He is a mature follower of Christ and lives out his faith daily. Al provides great leadership for the orphanage, and BGM has a wonderful relationship with the Children of Christ Home.

Today, 15 children live in the orphanage, and there is room for 18 more. Each child has his or her own bed. Each child gets three meals a day, a scholarship to a nearby school, and lots of love. Devotions are held daily for the children.

Two young American females, Rachel Charpie and Meredith Billings, who were recent college graduates, moved to Haiti and lived at the orphanage for two years. They helped coordinate the activities of the children, especially the educational process, and worked with visiting American teams who were interested in helping at the orphanage. Early on, an Occupational Therapist from Pensacola spent a week evaluating each child mentally and physically and prepared a notebook for each child with concrete steps to help the children develop as well as possible. The goal is for each child to go to a university and become a self-supporting, productive, godly member of the Haitian society. And then give back!

After two years, Meredith moved back to the States and Rachel took a new position with BGM. After that, Nash and Emily Barber, a young couple from Madison, MS moved to Haiti and worked at the orphanage for two years.

I WAS THINKING . . .

Say yes. Just say yes. Y.E.S. Yes. I know it's kind of scary. I know people will think you're crazy. But go ahead. Say it. Say yes.

The question? It doesn't matter. The details? Irrelevant.

And therein lies the challenge. Most of us want God to tell us His plan for our lives, complete with all the details, and then we'll decide if we want to go along. We'll then talk to our friends, weigh the pros and cons, and decide if that's what we want to do. There's just one problem with this approach: it's not how God works.

God doesn't want our approval for His plan. He wants our obedience to His plan. Let me repeat. God doesn't want our approval for His plan. He wants our obedience to His plan.

You see, if we wait until we know all the details, then it's not faith. It's sight. Sight is not always bad, it's just not faith. And remember, without faith it is impossible to please God.

What did He tell Abraham? "Pack everything up and move to a new land." Where is it, Lord? "I'll show you on the way."

The disciples? "Come follow me." How's that for details?

If we're not careful, we'll spend our entire lives waiting. We'll wait until the timing is perfect. Until the money is all there. Until we know precisely how it's going to turn out. We'll just wait. And while we wait, we miss out. We miss out on what God had planned for our lives. We miss out on the incredible ways He wanted to use us and bless us and show us His glory. We miss Him providing and helping and demonstrating His strength and His power and His love. We miss it all because we refused to exercise faith. We refused to trust. We refused to believe.

So what do we do? We tell him yes. We say, "God, I know you're doing something in my life. I'm not sure exactly what it is. But the answer is yes. I'll do it. I'll go. I'll pray and read and study and seek to determine your plan. But now, today, before I know all the details, the answer is yes."

CHAPTER 4

Transition Time

In June, 2011, shortly after we began construction of the sustainable community in Haiti, I became eligible for a six week sabbatical at First Baptist Jackson. For many months prior to my sabbatical, I had sensed it might be time to leave the church and pursue other ministry options. After leading that congregation for seven and a half years, I had begun to believe it would be good for the church and good for me if another pastor came to provide fresh leadership. In fact, I wrote the following in my journal on August 23, 2010, as I traveled to Haiti for the first time to see the tent cities:

> Not sure what to do next. At some point I will know with certainty that God has released me from First Baptist Jackson. But I do not want to move from Madison. Jewell and I love it there. But we will always be obedient to where He wants us. I have pastored 3 different type churches: (1) rural church, (2) medium sized county-seat church, and (3) large mega-church in a downtown setting. I've done those things and enjoyed them. Wondering what God wants from me next. Maybe I'll learn something on this trip.

Almost one year later, on August 14, 2011, I preached my final sermon as the Senior Pastor of First Baptist Jackson. We held one service and the sanctuary was packed with 3,000 people present. Both side balconies were full and folding chairs were placed in the back. We had a full orchestra and over 250 voices in the sanctuary choir. Childhood friends from my hometown of Natchez, Miss. were there. Friends from previous pastorates were there. My parents were there. As I concluded my sermon, the congregation stood and applauded. It was a big day.

That afternoon, there was a reception in the Fellowship Hall. Over 800 people came. Many waited an hour or more to say goodbye. Jewell and I stood in a reception line and shook hands and hugged necks for three solid hours without a break. It was really overwhelming. Countless cards and notes were left for us in a basket. In fact, it took me three hours of continuous reading the next morning to go through all the cards and letters. As I wrote in my journal the following day, "The church really stood tall on Sunday. It was a great demonstration of their love and goodness."

One of the most significant things that happened for But God Ministries and the work in Haiti took place that day at the end of my final service at First Baptist Jackson. Following the sermon, invitation, and announcements, my family went to lunch. The rest of the church stayed and entered into a Business Meeting. Then, the church voted overwhelmingly to pay my salary and health benefits for one year so I could establish a 501(c)(3), non-profit organization to continue the work in Haiti. We would have a separate, independent Board of Directors, and I would be the Executive Director of the organization.

I am thrilled to report the plan worked. The provision of my salary and health benefits for one year allowed me to work exclusively on setting up the organization and getting it on solid ground. At the end of that first year, But God Ministries was financially stable, the work was going in an amazing way, and the organization began paying my salary.

I would be less than candid if I did not share some of my feelings and struggles about leaving First Baptist Jackson. Serving that historic church for almost eight years was a great honor. It offered an incredible platform through its history, location, membership, and statewide and national television audience to share the gospel of Jesus Christ. There were over 5,000 members, and twice during my tenure we had over 2,500 in Sunday School. The history of the church was significant. The pastor who preceded me had once been named by Time magazine as one of the seven most outstanding Protestant preachers in America. Approximately 700,000 square feet of space had been built at the Downtown Campus which is located directly across the street from the State Capitol. Over 15,000 people come each Christmas for the special Christmas production.

Every Sunday I preached before two former governors, the Chief Justice of the State Supreme Court, the Attorney General for the state, the statewide Commissioner of Agriculture, numerous state Senators and House members, and, when he was in town, one of our two United States Senators. That U.S. Senator joined while I was serving, and his Secret Service detail was standing nearby, complete with dark sunglasses, as the Senator and his wife united with the church. In addition, there was a Who's Who of successful business people who were members of the church. We once counted 125 doctors in the congregation. The joke around the church was that the safest place to get sick was at First Baptist Jackson on a Sunday morning. There were also more lawyers than we could count. Interestingly, most of these well-known members were very active in the life of the church. They attended regularly, gave generously, and participated in the ministries of the congregation. Of course, there were many more people who were not as well known or accomplished, but First Baptist

Jackson seemed to have had an unusual percentage of highly accomplished members.

While there were many wonderful qualities of the church, there were also many challenges. There was an antiquated organizational structure with 300 deacons who attended a monthly meeting. It was like a small church's monthly business meeting. There were 27 people on the finance committee and 27 people on the personnel committee, all deacons.

The biggest challenge was the city of Jackson. From 1988 to 2008, the city had declined in population from 202,000 to 172,000. Crime and the perception of crime were issues. The roads were in need of repair, the water system was constantly breaking, and other infrastructure issues were working against the best interests of the city.

The issues faced by the city of Jackson impacted the church. By 2009, only 26% of the members of the church lived in the city of Jackson. Just six years earlier that number had been 40%. That was a rapid decline in the number of church members who lived in the city where the church was located. The majority of the members were driving a significant amount of time and distance to get to downtown Jackson each week. In addition, they were driving past very large and active suburban churches to get there.

In addition to the challenges with the city of Jackson, two other factors were occurring simultaneously: (1) different views between some of the leadership and me as to how we should move forward as a church and (2) the rapid growth of our work in Haiti.

As stated earlier, as far back as August 23, 2010, I sensed that God was releasing me from my assignment at First Baptist Jackson. Then, on June 27, 2011, shortly after starting construction on the new community in Haiti, I went on a scheduled six-week sabbatical. The night of July 12, I was with my family in Destin, Florida when I knew that it was time for me to resign and move on with my life and ministry. While walking alone on the beach that night, I remember thinking, "When first called into the pastorate, I got to experience God when it wasn't safe, when I didn't know what was going to happen, when all I could do was believe – in Him and His promises. I want to be out on that water again, sailing the ocean of faith, where it's not so safe, not so predictable, not so certain, because I know that is where I will meet Him again."

Then, on Sunday, July 24, 2011, I slipped into the church after the first service had started. There is a back entrance and a secret set of spiral stairs that leads into the Senior Pastor's office. At the end of that first service, I walked into the sanctuary, ascended the steps to the platform, stood behind the podium, and read my resignation letter. I repeated that process at the end of the second service.

The historical nature of the church made for an interesting situation with the press. My resignation made the front page of the statewide newspaper. That's crazy! A preacher resigned from a local church. Happens every week. But in this state and at that church, it made front page news. Moreover, numerous articles followed over the succeeding days. There was great speculation as to what had really happened. Political science professors from some of the state universities were interviewed as to why I had resigned. Some were sure there had been a moral failure or an ethical violation but, of course, none of those things were true. It was simply time for me to move on and transition into another area of ministry.

As mentioned earlier, the church had to vote on providing my salary and benefits for one year so we could establish the organization to continue the work in Haiti. It was a secret ballot vote, which meant people were free to vote the way they wanted to vote. While we were confident the vote would go well (and it did), we really had no idea what would happen. Moreover, with over 5,000 members, many of whom I did not know nor had even met, not everyone was happy with every decision that was made while I was the pastor. That's simply the way things operate when you get that many people together in one group.

So, as we drew closer to my last Sunday and the day on which the church would vote on the proposed severance package, I sent an email to some of my closest friends and supporters within the church. I had read a book about ministers who leave churches with great bitterness and anger. They become emotionally and spiritually crippled for many years. In light of that book, I wrote the following email to my friends on August 10, 2011 as my final Sunday at First Baptist Jackson approached:

Regardless of what happens with the vote Sunday morning (negative vote, partial vote, amended vote, or any other kind of vote), I have made a decision to embrace life with the positive joy that I always have and to simply do my part, work hard, and trust the Lord. As it turns out, it's a lot better that way! And pleasing to the Father! And defeating to the enemy!

Plus, I want my children to live with a dad who loves life and loves God and who is always looking backwards with a thankful heart and forward with wonderful anticipation. I want my wife to live with a husband who is positive and upbeat and looking forward to great years ahead.

Also, I really am excited about what God has in store. I refuse to live the rest of my life in a state of bitterness over the past. God has something in store and I want to experience it. There are so many opportunities to serve the helpless, love the hopeless, and make a BIG difference in this world and in the lives of hurting people. But, I know that cannot happen if I am a sour, bitter man.

Now, this doesn't mean I won't have my moments over the next few days and that I won't be disappointed if the vote doesn't go our way. The difference is that I won't be controlled by it. In fact, I plan on preaching a positive, upbeat sermon this Sunday, enjoying the rest of the week, and then worshiping on Sunday.

I really do believe Matthew 6:33. I really do believe Proverbs 3:5-6. He has been faithful thus far in my journey of life, and He will be faithful to the end!

I WAS THINKING . . .

Ordinary people. Like you. And me. Like your friends and neighbors. Your fellow church members. Just people. With a few gifts. A few talents. A few resources. It's ordinary people like us that God has used for thousands of years to bring about significant change. People like the boy David, the girl Mary, the fisherman Peter. As Richard Stearns wrote, "If the gospel is to be proclaimed, poverty defeated, racism overcome, the tide of AIDS turned back, or injustice challenged, it will be done by ordinary people like you and me" (*The Hole in our Gospel*).

Unfortunately, so many of us believe that God could never use us, that we have nothing to offer in His service. We wrongly believe that if we were smarter, or richer, or more skilled, or knew more important people, then we could do great and mighty things for God. Sadly, we refuse to engage. We refuse to get involved. We refuse to offer what we do have to the God who fed 5,000 with five loaves and two fish.

"But," we protest, "that's just a story. It's just an ancient little tale of Jesus feeding some hungry people." No, it's not! It's so much more than that. It is the perfect demonstration of how God can take that which is offered, no matter how seemingly insignificant, and do extraordinary things that make a real difference in the lives of hurting people.

But it will never happen. We will never see it. We will miss out on the great I AM using us in extraordinary ways if we do not offer to Him what we do have. Instead of lamenting or complaining about what we do not have, we simply need to offer Him what we do have. OUR gifts. OUR talents. OUR minds. OUR efforts. OUR resources. Instead of worrying about what we don't have or wishing we had what someone else has, we should simply offer to God what we do have, believing that He will take that and do great and mighty things that we never knew.

And yet we still protest saying, "but my gifts and talents and resources are so small, so slight, so insignificant." Remember, it's not about how small your gifts are. It's about how big your God is. Fortunately, it's about His power and His strength and His ability to make much of little.

So today, right now, let's stop focusing on what we don't have and start offering to God what we do have. Then, let's pray and work and do and believe that He will use us for His glory and the benefit of others. It's time, Christian. It's time to help that neighbor, start that ministry, work with those who are suffering, go on that mission trip, love the unlovely, minister to that hurting family, join those other Christians in that worthy cause. It's time. It's simply time. It's time to set the excuses aside, rally other Christians, and get the job done. Then, when we do, we will experience the incredible joy of being used by Him to see lives changed now and forever. And remember. That. Never. Gets. Old!

CHAPTER 5

Teammates

F ollowing my last Sunday at First Baptist Jackson on August 14, 2011, I rested a day or two and then began working on establishing the organization through which we would continue our work in Haiti. Based on all that had happened thus far, there was only one name we could go with: But God Ministries. We had seen God do so many incredible things. He had done the impossible when there was no other way. He had paved the way, provided the resources, and guided our steps. There was no other name we could use.

Two Christian lawyers, Doug Gunn and Joyce Hall, helped us with the incorporation of But God Ministries. Doug was a dear friend who had served as Chairman of the Deacons one of the years I was at First Baptist Jackson. Joyce was a member of Broadmoor Baptist Church in Madison, MS. Twenty-three years earlier when I was in law school in Jackson and Broadmoor was still located in Jackson, my wife and I joined Broadmoor and Joyce and her husband, Daniel, were the Sunday School teachers of our Young Couples class. Now, here we were all those years later, and Joyce was blessing us once again.

Once we were incorporated, Frank Betts, a partner with the Eubank and Betts accounting firm, helped us acquire our very important 501(c)(3) non-profit status with the IRS. That took about four months, and Frank did a fantastic job guiding us all the way.

During this time, we held our first Board meeting. I knew that selection of the members of the Board would be a key step in our work in Haiti. I asked seven people to join me on the Board. These were seven people who were very loyal, very trustworthy, very mission-minded, and very strong in their Christian faith. These were people with whom I had been involved previously in missions and ministry.

Buddy Huff became our Board president. Buddy was chairman of the Pastor Search Committee at First Baptist Jackson when I was called there in 2004. Other initial board members included Dr. Lee Cope, Billy Van Devender, Mark Rich, John Lewis, Barbara Gladney, Wayne Comans, and me.

Buddy Huff has played an important role in my life since the summer of 2003 when he first contacted me about going to First Baptist Jackson as their Pastor. Buddy is an encourager. He lifts people up with his words and his deeds. Some time ago, I wrote the following devotion about Buddy:

> I want to be like him. He's this guy who is always positive, always encouraging, always uplifting. Always. For the ten years I've known him, he's been this way. Always. Every conversation. Every encounter. Every time.
>
> And it's not just me. Turns out he's that way with everyone.
>
> I had a conversation with a mutual friend the other day who said, "he's the finest man I've ever met."
>
> I was compelled to reply, "if there's a better man walking this earth, I haven't met him."
>
> What's his secret? Why do so many feel this way about him? I think there are many reasons, but one of the more important ones is his tongue,

that tiny part of the body that is so strong and so powerful.

Somewhere along the way, he mastered it. Somewhere along the way, he realized he could use his tongue to build people up or tear them down. To be positive or negative. To uplift or destroy. And he's chosen the former. Every time.

Now don't be mistaken. He'll speak the truth. He'll speak the hard truth when it needs to be said. He'll address the tough issues. But he'll do so with wisdom and strength. He'll be calm during a raging storm. And that's why people like him. Why they want to be around him. Why they seek him out during the good times and the bad.

I think he must have read what a man named James wrote a long time ago. In fact, I'm sure of it. James wrote that the tongue is small, like a bit in the mouth of a large horse or a rudder on a big ship, but wields enormous power. He said it's like a small spark that can ignite an entire forest. That's how powerful the tongue is. That's how important our words are.

After watching this guy for a decade, I think he realized many years ago he could spend his time making a difference in people's lives, and he could do so with his words. He could speak hope and joy and love into people's lives. He realized he had the option to do that. And he decided that's what he would do.

After all these years, I'm beginning to realize I have the same option. And so do you. Like him, we can speak hope and joy and love into people's lives. We can encourage and uplift and strengthen. It's a choice. He made that choice. And my life is better, far better, because he did.

Our Board at But God Ministries has provided an enormous amount of support. As the Executive Director of the organization, I run the day to day operations of our work along with the staff at our headquarters in Ridgeland, MS. However, I am in constant communication with our Board through emails, calls, and texts. I visit with members of the Board regularly and solicit their advice on upcoming projects. Of course, the Board meets formally four times per year to officially approve important matters such as our annual budget and long-range plans, but we speak informally countless times throughout the year.

All members of the Board have been to Haiti, most of them numerous times. They have helped with medical-dental clinics, built houses, worked with children, coordinated visiting teams, and helped families move from tent cities into our new homes. They have served faithfully, with no compensation, and are making a huge, eternal difference in the lives of hurting Haitians.

One member of the initial Board played a pivotal role in the early days of BGM. When I left First Baptist Jackson in August of 2011, I worked primarily from my home office. As we began to grow rather rapidly, we needed an assistant and an office. John Lewis, a board member at that time, offered to give us the entire upstairs of his real estate office at no cost! We moved in and stayed there three years. John never charged a penny for those offices, and we were able to have a place of our own.

PARTNER CHURCHES

In the fall of 2010, I was in the middle of a three-year term on the Order of Business Committee for the Southern Baptist Convention. While in Nashville for a meeting, I had breakfast one morning with a fellow committee member. His name was Will Langford, and he was the pastor of Great Bridge Baptist Church in Chesapeake, Virginia.

Will asked me what I had been up to lately. I began telling him about our new work in Haiti. Will said he was really glad to hear about this because a lady in his church named Sandi Moseley had come to his office following the earthquake in Haiti to see how they could engage in ministry there. She had called the Virginia Baptist Convention and left a message but no one had ever called her back. I assured him that if she called me I would call her back!

A number of weeks later I was at the home of my parents in Petal, MS when my cell phone rang. It was Sandi. She told me about her interest in Haiti and wanted to know how they could be involved. We had a great conversation, and Sandi organized a mission trip from their church. They took their first trip to Haiti with us in 2011 and built the very first house we ever built. They've been to Haiti every year since then. I've preached at their wonderful church on numerous occasions. They've hosted Pastor Mathurin, one of our Haitian pastor friends, several times as well as our missionary, Rachel Charpie. They continue to be wonderful partners in the gospel.

Another church that has partnered with us for many years is First Baptist Church of Brandon, MS. Paul and Margaret Baggett have given leadership to all the trips they have taken with us to Haiti. Margaret may be the single most organized human that has ever lived! All of her trips are well planned to the last detail. They get more accomplished on one trip than I ever thought possible. For example, on a one-week trip in May of 2019, they did the following:

* Purchased and delivered 200 Creole Bibles and shared the gospel
* Built a classroom at the school in the village of Mathias
* Painted the house of one of our translators
* Built 14 benches for the church
* Built and delivered 4 desks to the Mathias school
* Built 6 desks for the Thoman school

* Built and delivered two beds and mattresses
* Built and delivered 8 tables and benches
* Built shelves for the Thoman school library
* Built shelves for the Hope Center kitchen, office, laundry room
* Put in new countertops for the island in the Hope Center kitchen
* Painted kitchen cabinets
* Conducted Motherhood Seminar for 20 pregnant ladies
* Conducted Men's Bible Study
* Conducted Women's Bible Study
* Helped with English class
* Participated in baptism of 10 new Christians at the river

In addition, First Baptist Brandon has always been interested in building church buildings so that communities will have a place to gather for worship and discipleship. They raised tens of thousands of dollars to build our first church in the village of Galette Chambon. Then, four years later, they did it again for a sanctuary in the village of Thoman. Worship and discipleship take place at these buildings multiple times every week of the year.

PERSONNEL

When we first started BGM, I was the only employee. However, the ministry progressed so quickly that I soon needed help. The first place I turned was to my former assistant, Cynthia Howell.

Cynthia and I had worked together for twelve years, 1999-2011. The first four years were at the Clarke-Venable Baptist Church in Decatur, MS. Cynthia's husband, Byron, is a pastor. As I was leaving Clarke-Venable to go to First Baptist Jackson, Byron was being called to a church near Jackson. I invited

Cynthia to come along with me to First Baptist. Nancy Dearman was already working as the ministry assistant for the Senior Pastor at First Baptist, so Cynthia became my assistant for research and presentations. Among other things, she prepared all my PowerPoints and other presentations for all my speaking engagements, including preaching on Sundays.

When Cynthia came to work at BGM, she immediately began to organize the office, our files, and processes involving mission trips. She answered the phone, talked with potential mission trip participants, and many other things. In addition, Cynthia got her son, J. C. Howell, to create a website for us. She also started handling the books for us using a church accounting system that she had used at Clarke-Venable. As you can see, Cynthia wore many hats and took our ministry to a new level.

The next big hire involved Rusty Hall as our Managing Director. I first met Rusty in 2012. We held an interest meeting after church at Broadmoor Baptist Church for people who were interested in going on a mission trip to Haiti. Rusty and his wife, Michelle, attended the meeting. Michelle was interested in going and serving as a nurse in our medical clinic. Rusty was not interested in going on the trip and was just accompanying Michelle to the meeting.

Rusty and Michelle sat near the front as I made my presentation. I had the feeling that Rusty was bored and was just waiting for the meeting to end so he could go to lunch. Then, I came to that point in my presentation where I talked about economic development. Immediately, Rusty perked up. As a businessman for 35 years, Rusty was very interested in job training and business creation. He had already been involved in business development in other countries with other Christian businessmen. When all was said and done, Rusty went on the trip in early 2013 with Michelle and the rest of the group from Broadmoor.

I also went on the trip with the group from Broadmoor. One

day, we took our entire group to the tent city in Port-au-Prince where we were interviewing ten families who were interested in moving out of the tent city and into one of the houses we had built in Galette Chambon. Somehow, we had made a terrible mistake and invited eleven families to the meeting instead of ten. I met with the eleven families plus the group from Broadmoor in a small wooden structure there in the tent city. I explained what we were offering and what our expectations would be of those families who might move into our community.

Then, after the meeting, I had to call the eleventh family to the side and explain that we had made a terrible mistake and invited too many families to the meeting. It was a horrible experience for everyone involved. I felt awful, and the family was devastated. They had come to the meeting believing they would be getting a new house and a new lease on life. They were desperate to move out of the horrendous conditions of that tent city. Now, here I was explaining that we did not have enough houses, and it would be a significant amount of time before we built another one.

Rusty and Michelle observed this meeting with the family. When we returned to the Hope Center, Rusty called me aside and said that he and Michelle would like to donate the funds to build that family a new house. Rusty had been deeply touched by the plight of that family. He and Michelle had the resources to help, and they chose to do so.

About a year after that trip to Haiti, in February of 2014, Rusty contacted me and wanted to meet for lunch. At that time, I knew we were at a pivotal point in the life of BGM. I knew that we needed help to expand our efforts. I also knew that I needed someone I could trust to talk with potential donors, senior pastors and mission pastors of churches, university deans and presidents, and others who were interested in partnering with us. I needed someone who could represent our organization in a positive light. Also, I needed someone with a business background who understood finances and organizational development. My background was in communication, law, and church life. I needed someone who had strengths, particularly from a financial and business standpoint, that I did not possess. I felt Rusty was that person. He was smart, had 35 years of business experience, understood finances, and had a mature faith in Christ. These were the characteristics we needed in a Managing Director. I thought Rusty was someone with whom I could partner and who could help us expand the ministry.

At the end of our lunch meeting I told Rusty I thought he should come work for us at BGM. Of course, Rusty already had a job with outstanding compensation with an international medical equipment company. He was in charge of the entire southeastern part of the country. Rusty's life was good, more than comfortable, and he enjoyed his work. So, when I told him that I thought he should quit his job and come to work with us, he told me that was not the purpose of the meeting that day. I told him I understood that, but that he should come to work with us anyway. He said he had not thought of that, and we left the meeting.

A week or so later we met once again at the same location. Rusty said he been thinking about what I said and the possibility of him coming to work for BGM. He had been praying about it and believed that was what God wanted him to do. I said, "Great! When do you want to start?"

He said he wasn't sure about that and there were many questions to consider before he could make that kind of decision.

I said, "I thought you said this is what God wants you to do." He said that's true but there was a lot to consider.

I said, "Well, if God has called you to do this, then it's a matter of obedience or disobedience. All the rest is just details." I got the feeling Rusty was not very happy with my comments. Nonetheless, he continued to pray, and after a number of weeks reached the conclusion that he wanted to leave his lucrative position in the business world and come work with BGM. In

July of 2014, Rusty informed his company that he would retire in December of that year and then begin working for BGM. In January of 2015, Rusty came to work for us.

The addition of Rusty to the staff of BGM proved to be a turning point in our work. I am only one person and can only be at one place at one time. Rusty had the ability to represent BGM before any person or any group necessary. He had the wisdom, maturity, and experience to do whatever was necessary to move the organization forward. He brought decades of experience in the corporate world. There were organizational decisions that needed to be made if we were to grow properly. He helped with budgeting. He helped develop a personnel manual. Rusty worked on health insurance and retirement plans for BGM employees. Though he is not a fundraiser, his efforts led to a significant growth in our revenues. His work allowed me to communicate more often and more effectively with donors and potential donors. His work caused others to be engaged in our mission, and that led to increased revenue. The first year Rusty was with us our revenue increased $429,000. The second year he was with us our revenue increased an additional $478,000. That's an increase of over $900,000 the first two years Rusty was with us. But God!

Eventually, Rusty took over the leadership position for our work in the Mississippi Delta. He oversees all personnel, finances, and ongoing projects in the Delta.

After spending an additional four years with me, Cynthia Howell decided it was time to retire. At that point, our revenue had increased dramatically and we knew we needed a full-time accountant. Julie Humphreys was working with my wife at the Mississippi Academy of Family Physicians. I had gotten to know Julie through my wife's work. I knew Julie to be smart and capable, and I also knew she was a CPA. We interviewed Julie, and she came onboard with us.

As a CPA, Julie was able to take our financial reporting to an entirely new level. In 2018 and 2019, Julie led us through a challenging but very important change of accounting systems. Our old system had been adequate when our organization was smaller and the revenues significantly less, but we got to the point where that system was simply not capable of handling what needed to be done and the potential that we saw before us.

Cynthia had been handling both the finances and the mission teams. With Julie coming on board to handle the finances, we needed someone to coordinate the mission trips. Because we had added a second location in Haiti, we were having about 66 trips each year to Haiti and 850 people on those trips. That takes an enormous amount of coordination and planning. Beth Rigney had gone on a mission trip with us and was interested in working at BGM. She came to the office, interviewed with us, and began volunteering.

Beth, however, did something that many people fail to do. She worked herself into a full-time job. Beth showed up on time. She had a great attitude. And, importantly, she solved problems. We had a problem with the online surveys we were conducting once team members had returned from their mission trips. We were getting responses from people about trips, but we were unable to tabulate those responses into one report. Thus, the information was almost useless. We told Beth about the problem. She went home that weekend and came back Monday morning with a report that tabulated all of the responses into one report. It was rather amazing. Then, she kept solving other problems.

At that point, we knew we wanted to keep Beth around, and we hired her as our full-time Mission Trip Coordinator. Beth did an incredible job in that role for a couple of years. She then became interested in communication and how we promote our work through social media, email newsletters, video, and other means. In 2019, we created the position of Director of Communication and Media for BGM and moved Beth into that position. Thereafter, we hired Annette Hall for the role of Mission Trip Coordinator. Annette was born in Jamaica, moved to the United States to attend college at Belhaven University, married Fred Hall about 25 years ago, and has been in the States ever since. Annette had taken several trips with BGM to Haiti, was very familiar with our work, and we thought she would be the perfect fit as our Mission Trip Coordinator.

Around the time we hired Beth as our Mission Trip Coordinator, our child sponsorship program began to grow. At that time, we had hundreds of children being sponsored at five schools in Haiti at $37 per month. Today, we sponsor almost 1,000 Haitian children. Of course, this takes an enormous amount of coordination and computer work to keep up with all the children and all the sponsors. The work was becoming too much for those in our office who had other responsibilities. That's when Jo Willett showed up. Jo is a retired Office Manager. She is highly organized, self-motivated, and a hard worker. Jo is not one to sit around being idle. Importantly, she had been to Haiti with us on a mission trip.

One day Jo came by our office and offered to volunteer. We thought about all the children being sponsored and how we needed some help. That's when Jo accepted the role of Child Sponsorship Coordinator. Jo comes to the office every Tuesday and updates all of the child sponsor information. There is no way we could keep up with this important ministry without the help of Jo Willett.

During the spring of 2018, I begin to see the need for a Development Director. We needed someone whose sole focus would be to raise funds for BGM. God had blessed greatly up to that point, as we normally received funds through individual gifts and mission trip fees. However, we were not tapping into family foundations, corporate foundations, and other funding sources. If we wanted to continue to grow, we needed further funding. Up until that point, I had been the primary fundraiser for BGM. I knew we needed a person who could focus solely on raising funds. I would continue to raise funds, but I also have many other responsibilities within the organization, including vision casting, programming, overseeing our work in Haiti, and representing the organization in a myriad of settings.

One day I shared with one of our board members, Rick Adams, that I was thinking about creating a position called Development Director. Rick said that he had been on the board of the March of Dimes for the state of Mississippi and he knew that the Executive Director was leaving that position and was looking for a similar position. Rick highly recommended her. Her name is Dina Ray.

I met with Dina and explained that we were looking for a fundraiser. Dina shared that she had been raising funds for years with March of Dimes. Unlike 98% of all people, she stated that she was not afraid to make the ask. Most people would rather write you a check than ask other people to write a check. For whatever reason, Dina does not mind asking people to give to a worthy cause. She then met with our Board President, Buddy Huff, and with Rusty Hall, our Managing Director. We hired her in September 2018. It was wonderfully refreshing to have someone whose sole purpose was to generate funds. In less than a year, Dina was able to generate several hundred thousand dollars, and the prospects are very bright for this position.

Another person who is playing an important role in the life of BGM is Abby Winstead. I have known Abby since she was in elementary school. Abby was in the same grade as my twin sons and was very close with my son, Neal. In high school and college, Abby went to Haiti many times for week-long mission trips. Then, she spent a summer or two as an intern. After graduating from Mississippi State University, Abby moved to Texas and earned a master's degree in public health from the University of North Texas. Thereafter, in the fall of 2018, Abby moved to Haiti to use her new degree and address issues of public health and how we can better serve the people where we work.

One person who must be mentioned is a Haitian named

Vladimir. Vladimir has been with us from the beginning. He is from the city of Carrefour, west of Port-au-Prince. He started translating for us as we began construction on the Hope Center in Galette Chambon in 2011. Vladimir has perfect English and understands slang words and phrases and even the southern dialect from the States. He is steady and trustworthy. In fact, Vladimir lives with Tony and Mickie in their house in the Hope Center. Thousands of Americans who have been to Haiti are friends with Vladimir.

I WAS THINKING . . .

They started walking at noon on Saturday. They left their crude mountain home because she had been struck in the head by a boulder. She was bleeding profusely. They walked continuously until it became dark and a storm erupted. Some kind people allowed them to stay the night in their mountain home, likely made of mud and sticks.

Yesterday morning they started walking again. At 9:00 a.m. they finally made it to The Hope Center and our medical clinic there in Haiti. Tony, our full-time American nurse, tended to her wounds, cleaned off the blood, stabilized her. He then realized her needs were greater than what we could provide because she had lost a tremendous amount of blood from the blow to her head and from walking for a day. So he drove her to a hospital in Port-au-Prince, paid for her medical care, and headed home.

At 6:00 p.m. yesterday the husband and wife and four year old girl arrived at The Hope Center. They live far in the mountains, a hard drive of 2 ½ hours from The Hope Center. A large tree limb had fallen on the girl, broken her arm, and gashed her head. They had used all their money to go to a trauma center in Port-au-Prince. The good doctors at the trauma center treated her arm but said they do not treat head wounds. Near the trauma center was a man who lives near our Hope Center. He told the little family about our clinic and gave them just enough money to get transportation.

Tony put 20 staples in the little girl's head. Then they told Tony they had no money and nowhere to go for the night. For the first time since April 7, we have no American team staying at The Hope Center. Tony invited them to take a shower, eat dinner, and spend the night in our dorm. They graciously accepted the offer. This morning Tony gave them money to get transportation home.

Between these two medical events, 6 precious children moved into our orphanage. They will not only get a good and safe roof over their heads, but they will receive medical care, dental care, clean water, plenty of food, clothing, a church, a new playground, and scholarships for school. They will learn about a wonderful God who loves them. And they will be loved. Every day.

I was thinking this morning that I am so glad our medical clinic is there. I was thinking how glad I am for the new orphanage. And I was wondering. I was wondering if God smiled as Tony cleaned wounds, gave transportation and money for more medical help, and sewed the head of that little girl. I was wondering how pleased God was as that family who had nothing took their showers, ate their meals, and slept on clean sheets.

And there was one other thing I was wondering this morning. As God watched Tony, did He think about that Samaritan who was so good? I know I did.

CHAPTER 6

The Right People at the Right Time

One of the things that has amazed me in our work in Haiti and the Mississippi Delta is the countless times God has sent the right people at the right time. Whenever there has been an issue, whenever there has been a challenge, whenever we weren't sure what to do, God has had the right person in the right place at the right time. It's happened over and over again.

One time we were having problems with one of our generators, and we weren't sure what to do. A team was working at the Hope Center at that time and one man said, "Excuse me, but I've been repairing generators for 26 years." He fixed the generator. But God!

Another time we were building the missionary house for the nurse and his family who would be moving to Haiti on a full-time basis. We needed cabinets built in the kitchen. We weren't sure what to do until we learned that a man coming with a mission team from Virginia the next week was President of the National Cabinetry Association. That's right, President of the National Cabinetry Association. You couldn't make this stuff up! His name is Dave Alderman. We call him Super Dave! He came, built the cabinets in the missionary house, and then tore out and rebuilt cabinets in the main kitchen of the Hope Center. But God!

Another time we were constructing the church. We had come to a critical point in the construction process in which we had completed the foundation and the walls and it was time to build the roof. This was the largest building we had every built with a much larger roof span than we had ever attempted. We had American architects who had designed the building but we were in Haiti with a Haitian contractor using Haitian materials and Haitian workers. So, what did God do? The very week that it was time to start construction of the roof, a man came on a mission team. This man was Jim Gorrie. Jim is President and CEO of one of the largest privately held construction companies in America with over 3,000 employees and offices in many cities. This man and his company have built skyscrapers, stadiums, hospitals, mega-churches, and countless other buildings. Jim "just happened" to be on a mission trip with one of our teams at the very moment we needed to move forward on the construction of the church. He offered sound guidance to our construction supervisor, gave great advice on both design and implementation, and the work went forward in a proper way. But God!

Some of my favorite people in all the world are Mike and Jann Kenney. They are married to one another and they are plumbers. Mike had been a plumber for a number of years when he married Jann. At that time, Jann was working in a high-end position in the medical field. Jann loved Mike so much she quit her job in the medical field and joined Mike as his assistant so they could spend more time together.

As we began construction of the Hope Center, we knew we had to have running water for our medical-dental clinic, for our teams that would be staying there each week, and for the missionary house where our American nurse and his family would be living. But there we were on a plain in a rural area in the middle of nowhere. So, we drilled a well and hit water. Then, Mike and Jann volunteered to come to Haiti and plumb all of our buildings. They ran water lines to our two clinic buildings, the kitchen, the bathrooms, and the missionary house. They installed 7 sinks, 5 toilets, 3 showers, and 1 septic tank system. All of this took place over 5 different volunteer trips Mike and Jann made to Haiti within one year. And there's one thing to remember about Mike and Jann - they are self-employed plumbers. They are not on salary, so when they are not working in the States they are not receiving any income. But they volunteered anyway, losing five weeks of income. FIVE WEEKS! Every time I take a shower or flush a toilet or wash my face or use water in any way at the Hope Center, I thank God for Mike and Jann.

Then there was the electrician. He has worked for over 20 years for the Jackson Public School System doing electrical work in their countless number of buildings. He learned about our work and volunteered to take vacation time to go to Haiti and wire our buildings. All of them - the two clinics, the dorm, the kitchen/bathrooms, and the missionary house. Thanks to the generators, the intermittent electricity from the nearby town, an automatic transfer switch, and an electrician from Jackson, MS, we have electricity whenever we want it.

On December 10, 2011, four months after I resigned from First Baptist Jackson, I received a phone call from Texas. I answered my phone and the man on the other end of the line said, "I'm looking for Stan Buckley."

I said, "You've found him. This is Stan. To whom do I have the pleasure of speaking?"

He said, "My name is Bobby, and my wife and I used to watch you every Sunday on Directv. Then you left, and we weren't sure what happened to you." He continued, "I've been looking everywhere for you. Finally, the other day I was at a horse auction here in Texas. A man bought some of the horses I was selling. I walked up into the stands to try and find the man and thank him for buying my horses. As I walked up the stairs, a young man was standing in the aisle. I asked him if he saw the man who had just bid on my horses. They young man pointed out the man who had made the bid. Then I started talking to the young man. He told me he was from Mississippi. I asked where in Mississippi, and he said Jackson. I told him I was looking for a preacher named Stan Buckley, and I was wondering if he knew you. He said he not only knew you, but you had been his pastor. Then, he reached into his wallet and handed me your business card. He said he had run into you at a restaurant a few days earlier and you had given him your business card. And that's how I got your number."

What are the odds of Bobby meeting a guy from Mississippi at an auction in Texas who had my business card in his wallet? Bobby and his wife, Dottie, went on to become active in our work in Haiti and the Mississippi Delta, and I wrote part of this book from a guest house they own at a ranch in Texas. But God!

I WAS THINKING . . .

I wish I had some more. A lot more. If I did, I could really help people. I could make a difference in their lives. If I just had some more. You know, money. But since I don't, I can't help people. After all, that's the only thing people need.

They don't need encouragement. Or love. Or care or concern or wise counsel. They don't need a friend or a smile or a compliment. They don't need a recommendation for a job or a pat on the back or a listening ear. Or do they?

I'm so glad those two guys didn't walk away from that crippled man because they didn't have any money. The crippled man was begging for money, and the two guys didn't have any. But they had something he really needed. So, they gave it to him. They gave him Jesus. The one named Peter said, "Silver or gold I do not have, but what I have I give you. In the name of Jesus of Nazareth, walk." And he did.[1]

The truth is that money can be used for good and noble purposes. It can be used to help people in real and tangible ways. So, if you have money, give it. Bless people with it. Change their circumstances. Give them a hand-up.

But if you don't have money, you can still give. Boy, can you give! Give them hope and joy and peace. Give them a friend and a future and a focus. Give them meaning. And purpose. And a life that matters. Today, in the middle of their sorrow and their struggles and their hopelessness, give them what you have. Give them Jesus.

---

[1] Acts 3:6 – NIV translation

Stan Buckley

CHAPTER 7

Lifeblood

The lifeblood of our work consists of the teams that go to our Hope Centers each week to minister in the name of Jesus. They go to offer help and hope. The go to love and bless. They encourage the Haitian people, the people of the Mississippi Delta, and our American staff. Most of them are from churches, though not all of them. The teams and individuals come from all across the United States, though the majority tend to be from the south. We have had teams from Oregon, Colorado, Oklahoma, Arkansas, Louisiana, Mississippi, Tennessee, Florida, Alabama, Georgia, South Carolina, and Virginia. We have had individuals from all those states plus Texas, Ohio, Wisconsin, New Jersey, Illinois, Missouri, and more.

Most of our teams are multi-functional in nature. Some of the team members conduct medical clinics. Some conduct dental clinics. Some lead Ladies Bible Studies and Vacation Bible School. Some work with the children in the orphanage. Some preach in nearby churches. Some do construction work. Some lead Family Night in which we invite families who have moved into our houses to come to The Hope Center at night and just have fun, play games, or watch a movie. Family Night builds community and blesses all who attend.

One of my favorite conversations about Haiti took place on a flight from Port-au-Prince to Miami. I was sitting across the aisle from a tall, striking, Haitian lady. As we talked, I learned that her father had been the mayor of the second largest city in Haiti when the dictator, Baby Doc, was overthrown many years earlier. This lady was seven years old at the time, and her family thought they might be killed in the revolution so they fled to Miami. The lady did not return until eleven years later when she was 18 years old. A number of years later she married a Haitian man. He lives in Haiti, and she maintains her home in Miami and goes back and forth regularly. She then explained to me that she has a small non-profit organization in which she helps with a school and an orphanage in Haiti.

Then the lady asked me what I was doing in Haiti. I told her about our work and explained that we have doctors and dentists and nurses who come to Haiti to work in our clinic. She then asked a question I was not expecting. She said, "How much do you have to pay the medical people to come to Haiti?" I said, "We don't pay them anything. In fact, they volunteer their time and their skills and they pay us to cover their expenses."

She was in shock. She couldn't believe it. She said, "No, really, how much do you pay them?"

I repeated what I had told her. "Honestly, we don't pay them anything. Not only that, we have another 300 people who come to Haiti to do other kinds of work such as construction or electrical work or plumbing work. Some help with Bible studies and Bible school. Some do agriculture work. They do all kinds of things."

She said, "How much do you pay them?"

I said, "We don't pay them anything. They take off from work, buy their plane tickets, and pay us to cover their expenses."

She couldn't believe it. She said, "I can't get three people to volunteer, and I live in Miami!"

I said to her, "You're asking the wrong people. The people who volunteer with us are Christians who love the Lord and who love His people. They believe it is their duty and their privilege to serve others in God's name." And I told her, "You need to find some Christians to ask. They are the ones who will love and serve and bless. They're the ones who will go and help and minister. You need to ask the right people."

In that moment, I had never been so proud of God's Church, the Body of Christ. In that moment, I knew the Church was alive and well. I knew that every week I get to see the Church do what the Church is supposed to do – share the gospel, love the hopeless, minister to the needy. I knew that while many condemn the Church today, sometimes rightfully so, the Church of Jesus Christ is still busy serving and loving and helping and sharing. I knew the Church was shining brightly in Haiti, and the name of Jesus is being lifted high every day.

You see, that was the greatest witness I could give to that Haitian lady at that time. She was amazed that all these Christians would give and go and sacrifice for the people of her country. No one else was going. She couldn't find anyone to help her worthwhile cause. But when I told her about all these Christians traveling to her country, she knew something was different. She knew they had a different kind of love. I was thrilled to tell her of the great love of God's people.

I have come to learn over the last eight years that it's in serving the poor and the hopeless, the widows and the orphans, the outcasts and the hurting, that we are most like our Christ. It's in those times we are fulfilling both the commands and the examples of Jesus.

The sad truth is that in so many of our churches we American Christians spend a huge amount of our time on things that don't matter, things that don't help share the gospel, things that don't minister to the ones Jesus said we should minister. We go to meetings, we give our money, we argue about color-of-the-carpet issues that don't make a bit of difference in the Kingdom of God, but we neglect those things that matter.

As I travel and speak at many different churches, I am discovering that people are tired of those things. They are tired of fussing and fighting over things that don't matter. They are tired of the same ole, same ole. They have come to realize that life really is a vapor and they want what little time they have on this earth to matter. They want it to count. They want their lives to make a difference in the lives of others. They want to be used by God in great and mighty ways for His glory and for the benefit of others. No longer will they be content to just "do church." No longer will they engage in endless discussions and squabbles about things that simply do not matter, that make no difference in anyone's life.

Week after week, we see people at our Hope Centers who have resolved to make a difference in this world. It's so exciting! It's so encouraging! And it's making a difference. A HUGE difference!

I WAS THINKING . . .

So what? So what that you weren't the smartest in your class. Or the most popular. So what that you don't have a zillion dollars in the bank. So what there are people who are more educated or better looking or have better connections. Are those the things God is looking for?

That doesn't seem to be what set those guys apart on that day long ago. Yet everyone could see it. It was as plain as day. They had courage. They stood tall. They were neither afraid nor ashamed. And they changed lives. Who could deny it?

It would make more sense if they had been highly educated. A college degree, perhaps a Master's, would have given them a leg up. Some special skill would have set them apart. But no. They were unschooled and ordinary. Not much education. Nothing special about them.

And yet, there they were. Teaching and preaching and drawing large crowds. And then there was the miracle where that crippled man stood up and started running around. No one could deny that. But how could those two guys do it? They were unschooled. And ordinary. They were just two regular Joes. Or one regular Peter and one regular John. Yep, Peter and John. Unschooled and ordinary.

So how did they do it? Was it their lack of education or their plain lives? Not exactly. Turns out there was one other thing. And those around them noticed. In fact, other people "took note that these men had been with Jesus."[2]

That's it. That's the difference. That's what set them apart and gave them the courage and the strength to do amazing things that would make a huge difference in this world. They had been with Jesus. Spent time with. Listened. Loved. Obeyed. They had experienced His grace and His love and His power.

---

[2] Acts 3:6 – NIV translation

They had known His peace and His joy. They had been with Jesus and it changed everything.

Unschooled and ordinary. That's who God is looking for. Ordinary folks who are willing to serve an extraordinary God. That way, when God does an amazing work, no one has to wonder who did it. God gets the credit. People look to Him rather than us. And that's a lot better since hope and joy and peace are found in Him and not in us.

A guy named Paul once wrote that, "God chose the foolish things of the world to shame the wise; God chose the weak things of the world to shame the strong. He chose the lowly things of this world and the despised things – and the things that are not – to nullify the things that are, so that no one may boast before him." [3]

So today if you're feeling weak and ordinary or not-so-special, you're in pretty good company. You're the one He wants to use for His glory and the benefit of others. So take heart. Be encouraged. Launch out in faith to serve Him boldly. And oh yeah, before you go, make sure you have "been with Jesus."

[3] 1 Corinthians 1:27-29 – NIV translation

CHAPTER 8

Spheres

During the first two years of our work in Haiti, we narrowed our focus to a number of areas, or SPHERES, in which we operate. We realized there are certain basics in life that all people, regardless of location, need. These basics include things such as food, water, shelter, medical care, a church, a job, and an education. Everyone on the planet needs access to these items. We call these items, or areas, SPHERES. These SPHERES include the flowing areas:

   S – spiritual
   P – physical (medical/dental)
   H – H2O
   E – education
   R – roofs (housing)
   E – economic development (jobs)
   S – Soil (access to healthy food)

The first two areas of our work, spiritual and physical, are of great importance. However, it seems that over the years Christians have gone to one extreme or the other. Some have focused on the spiritual needs to the exclusion of the physical needs. They will share the gospel, hand out tracts, engage in evangelistic efforts, and get someone to say a prayer of repentance. All the while, the person has no house, no food, and no clean water.

On the other side of the coin, some Christians have focused on the physical needs to the exclusion of the spiritual needs. They will provide housing and food and clean water, but never address the deep needs of the soul. They never bother to tell the person he is loved by a wonderful God who sent His Son to die on a cross so that he might have forgiveness of sins, hope, the abundant life, and life eternal.

As we read the Scriptures and examine the work of our Lord, we learn that the spiritual and the physical were not two separate ministries of Jesus. They were one and the same. While feeding people bread and fish, He talked about love, grace, and forgiveness. While healing the blind, the deaf, and the leprous, He talked about the Kingdom of God, mercy, and hope. Jesus struck an amazing balance between the physical and the spiritual. We strive to do the same.

SPIRITUAL

The spiritual aspect of our work is of utmost importance. As a certain pastor from Florida once said, "we are not trying to simply make a better place for people to go to hell from." We believe it is our responsibility, as well as our great privilege, to address the spiritual needs of the people of Haiti.

The greatest need of every person is salvation. We are all sinners in desperate need of a Savior. We believe all people have sinned and fallen short of the glory of God, and the punishment for sin is death – both physically and spiritually in a terrible place called hell. But we also believe that is not the end of the story. We believe the gift of God is eternal life through Jesus Christ our Lord. We believe Jesus Christ, the Son of God, is the Savior we so desperately need. The Bible teaches that God loved this world so much "that He gave His one and only Son, that whoever believes in Him should not perish but have eternal life." [4] We believe Jesus lived a sinless life, died a sacrificial death on a cross, and rose from the dead defeating Satan and death and hell.

We believe when a person turns from his sins and embraces Jesus Christ through faith, that person becomes a new creation in Christ. He is born again. He receives the gift of eternal life. With that gift come hope and joy, redemption and love, peace and purpose. This is the Good News we share with the people of Haiti.

How do we go about addressing the spiritual needs of those Haitians we encounter? What is our primary strategy for evangelism and discipleship? Our main strategy is NOT to wait for Americans to show up every few weeks to hold a worship service. We want evangelism and discipleship to be an ongoing, daily process. In addition, like everything else we do in Haiti, we want the spiritual work to be sustainable. Therefore, our primary spiritual strategy involves partnering with Haitian pastors for the communities we are building. Our plan is to have well-trained, educated, Haitian pastors with servant-hearts who live in the sustainable communities and serve the entire communities as pastors.

To this end, we initially partnered with Pastor Daniel. Pastor Daniel is a graduate of the same seminary from which I graduated – New Orleans Baptist Theological Seminary. New Orleans seminary had a branch in Port-au-Prince that offered a two year program in Pastoral Ministry. Pastor Daniel completed this program and moved to our community to be the pastor of the church we established. He preached in the new church building every Sunday and Wednesday and held Bible studies throughout the week. He led in all aspects of church ministry, including worship, ministry, missions, fellowship, and discipleship.

---

[4] John 3:16 – NIV

After a couple of years, Pastor Daniel married and moved to the States. We then called Pastor Mickenson to be the Pastor of the church. Pastor Mickenson is an enormously talented man with an exceptional singing voice. He and his wife and young son moved to the Hope Center and served at the church for a couple of years. Since they left to return to the city, we have had an interim pastor.

While having a Haitian pastor in the community is our primary strategy for meeting spiritual needs, we have also been engaging people in other ways: by sharing the gospel with those who come to our medical-dental clinic, by holding Ladies Bible Studies, by hosting Vacation Bible Schools for children, by showing the Jesus Film, by meeting physical needs, and by one-on-one sharing of the hope that is within us. These and other means are used to share the love of Jesus Christ and the Good News of the Gospel.

VOODOO PRIEST

Voodoo is alive and well in Haiti. It is practiced by numerous people. Voodoo is a very dark religion. It enslaves people and binds people and keeps them from having the life God would have for them. Mostly, it keeps them from knowing Jesus Christ and having both the abundant life and eternal life that He promised.

There are numerous voodoo priests in the village where we work in Galette Chambon, Haiti. We have shared the hope of the gospel with them many times. Leaving their role as a voodoo priest would not only present them with spiritual challenges but also financial challenges. They often receive money for placing curses on people. For example, if I were mad at you, I would go to the voodoo priest and pay him to put a curse on you.

One of the voodoo priests in our village was arrested. He

was in jail for about six months and prayed to Satan and other false gods to be released. However, he was never released. Finally, he decided to pray to this Jesus that he had always heard about. Upon praying, he was released from prison the same day. He immediately went to our Hope Center and banged on the gate. He came in and asked to speak to our Haitian pastor who was living in the Hope Center at that time.

Our pastor's name was Mickenson. Mickenson shared the gospel with the voodoo priest, and he was saved. He committed his life to Christ. The next day, Sunday, the now former voodoo priest showed up for the worship service at our church. At the end of the service, he made public his decision to leave voodoo and embrace Christ. After the service, he invited the mission team that was there to accompany him back to his part of the village. Upon arriving, he asked them to help him tear down the hut where he performed many of his voodoo rituals. He threw it all on the ground, including the idols. Then, he set the entire thing on fire! It was a glorious day for him, our team, our missionaries, and the kingdom of God!

PHYSICAL

There are enormous physical needs in Haiti. The primary means by which we seek to meet those physical needs is through our medical-dental clinics. We have treated tens of thousands of people at our two clinics.

Our first clinic was open four days per week when a visiting medical-dental team was not present. Tony West, our resident American nurse practitioner and Medical Director, operated the clinic Monday, Tuesday, Thursday, and Friday. He used Wednesday as a day to engage in administrative work.

Whenever we have a visiting American medical-dental team, we see patients 5 or 6 days per week. In addition to seeing patients at our clinic buildings in The Hope Center, we often conduct mobile clinics during the week in remote villages that have no access to health care. We have seen upwards of 1,700 patients in a week when we have large teams. Some medical-dental teams are small with one doctor, a nurse practitioner, and one dentist. Other teams are larger with two pediatric dentists, an oral surgeon, a cardiologist, an internist, two nurse practitioners, and ten dental students.

In February 2013, we had our first birth at The Hope Center. A mom that had been coming to the Hope Center for checkups during her pregnancy appeared and said she thought it was time for her baby to be born. Tony took her into the clinic building and prepared the room for the birth. Shortly thereafter her water broke. Then nothing. Finally, the lady said she was going to walk around the courtyard outside the clinic building. Tony began seeing other patients until one of the security guards entered the clinic and told him he thought the lady was about to give birth. Tony told him to bring the lady into the clinic. The security guard said he thought it was too late for that. Tony quickly went outside to find the lady on the ground giving birth! There was not even enough time to walk 20 steps into the clinic. Within minutes, a beautiful little girl was born. Her name? Hope. And to top it off, 20 minutes after giving birth, the lady picked up her baby and walked home! Since then, over 500 babies have been born at our clinics, including one set of twins.

One evening at the Hope Center it was dark, and we had just finished eating dinner when we heard a banging at the main gate. The door was opened, and a lady stumbled into the Hope Center. She could barely walk and was being supported by friends and family members on each side. The lady's 18 day old baby was with them.

The friends took the lady to the clinic. Tony immediately went to see what was wrong. He had planned to check her blood pressure, but as he touched her arm she felt extremely hot. He started taking her temperature but quit when it got to

104 degrees. This was serious! He then put ice on her body and started a drip.

After getting her settled and working on her high temperature, Tony called a doctor from Hattiesburg, MS who had been at the Hope Center the week before. He described to the doctor the symptoms of the lady and how he was treating her. The doctor concurred with Tony's treatment. Then, the doctor said to Tony, "Based on everything you have told me, if the clinic was not there, and if she were not receiving the medical care you are now providing, she would likely be dead." This lady lived more than an hour's drive away in a remote village.

An additional blessing that night was the fact that we did not have a team there, and the dorm was not being used. We brought food left over from our evening meal and gave it to the three friends and family members. They were hungry and grateful. Then we told them their friend was going to have to spend the night, and they were welcome to stay in our beds in the dorm. So, after a good meal and after seeing that their loved one was going to be okay, they settled in for a good night's sleep. The next day the lady's temperature was 98.6, and she left the Hope Center physically drained but doing much better.

One morning a Haitian man appeared at the clinic with a big problem. He had a mouth filled with hurting teeth. It was 7:00 a.m., and he had been walking five hours to arrive at the clinic, having left his village at 2:00 that morning. We thank God the clinic was open, and the man had five teeth pulled. He was a little sore, but he was happy when he left.

While we were thrilled beyond measure to have Tony operating the clinic on a daily basis and hosting medical-dental teams from America, we still wanted to meet the physical needs of Haitian people in a way that was as organic and sustainable as possible. To that end, we hired a Haitian doctor, Haitian nurse, Haitian lab tech, and Haitian pharmacy tech. Now, even when our missionaries are out of the country, the clinic continues to function and treat patients. We know that our Haitian staff has a full understanding of the language, culture, and medical needs of the people. They are Haitian medical personnel treating Haitian patients. They are Haitian providers who are fully employed. This is yet another step in the development of a sustainable community.

CLINIC EXPANSION

Our clinic in GC was doing great. We were seeing thousands of patients and meeting many needs. However, the clinic consisted of only two buildings and no decent waiting room. In fact, the people had to wait outside in the sun or the rain. We thought we could do better than that. So, we designed a clinic expansion that would include a lab, a room for triage, four exam rooms, two toilets, and two showers. In addition, there would be a large covered waiting area to keep people out of the sun and the rain.

Once again, we had no funds to build the expansion. The cost was going to be approximately $50,000. One day I was talking to my friend Craig Beatty from Birmingham, Alabama. Craig had been to Haiti a couple of times and was very supportive of our work. He owns a successful construction company. I told him what we were trying to accomplish, and he invited me to his office in Birmingham to share about the plans for the expansion. He said he had some friends who are in the construction business and might want to help out. He would invite them to the meeting.

Several weeks later I showed up in Birmingham to meet with Craig and his friends. Craig had lunch brought in, I set up my computer with the PowerPoint presentation, and Craig's friends begin to arrive. At that time, Jim Gorrie walked into the room. Craig and his friends all know Jim from the construction business. Jim has one of the largest companies in the southeast and is well respected by all the others. His presence and affirmation provided great credibility for BGM and me as I made the presentation. After a few questions, I left to drive home to Mississippi. On the way home, Craig called to tell me that several of the guys were donating $10,000 each. It was a blessed day and we had most of the funds to build the expansion. But God!

One of the best parts of the expansion was the space for a new lab. The lab was desperately needed. At that time we could only examine the patient and tell the patient what we thought was the diagnosis. We would then have to send the patient to a lab to get confirmation. That was more challenging than one can imagine. We would have to give the patient a little money and hope they could make it to a lab somewhere outside the community. We hoped the lab would be open, and they could be seen. Then they would have to wait for the results. Sometimes that took days. We then hoped they would go back to the lab and bring the results to us. That could take weeks in Haiti, and all of the steps had to fall into place perfectly for us to get the results back. It was not a good system.

So, we raised the funds for the lab equipment and opened the lab. It has been a game-changer for us. We can now examine the patient, test the patient on the spot, and get a proper diagnosis. We can then treat the patient for what we know to be the problem. All of this can take place in one visit by the patient. In addition to helping our patients, we hired a full-time lab tech who now has a job. Everyone wins!

EMR

When we opened the clinic, our patient records were kept on pieces of paper. We filed them manually. After seeing thousands and thousands of patients, this became unwieldy and ineffective.

One day, Tony West was talking with some mission team members from Pensacola about the need for an electronic medical records system. We had looked at some systems in the United States where most of them were cloud-based. It was difficult to find one that was not cloud-based.

Matt Johnson, a member of the Pensacola team, overheard Tony's discussion with the other team members.

He said, I can make you an electronic medical records system." Tony said, "That would be great!"

As it turns out, Matt is brilliant. Really smart. He works on humanoid robots. So, he went home and created an electronic medical records system that we could use in our clinics in Haiti. This system has greatly enhanced our ability to deliver quality healthcare. Now, a patient comes to the clinic for the first time, checks in, and is given a laminated card with his name and a special number. Thereafter, whenever he comes to the clinic and checks in, we type his number into our system. Then, his entire medical history appears on the screen. It shows when he last visited, which doctor he saw, the nature of his problem, the diagnosis, and the medicine that was prescribed.

Every medical person in our clinic in the chain of care has a computer with the electronic medical records system on it. They are all connected through Wi-Fi. So, after the patient checks in, he goes to a nurse to get his blood pressure and other vital signs checked. She records it immediately into the electronic medical records system. When the patient goes to see the doctor, she pulls up his records and sees his past visits as well as the numbers for his vital signs. Also, the pharmacy can pull up a patient's records and see what was prescribed by the doctor.

In January 2019, we installed the electronic medical records system at our second clinic which is in Thoman, Haiti. Once again, this is changing how we are able to deliver quality healthcare.

H2O

Clean water is necessary for healthy, successful lives. Whether we live in Houston, Honolulu, or Haiti, without water we will die quickly. With unsanitary water, we will contract all manner of diseases and be continuously sick.

In Haiti, like other developing countries, the challenge is not only the condition of the water, but also the location of the water. Many Haitians spend a great amount of time each day walking to acquire water. When they finally get the water, transportation of the water becomes an issue. First, the water is often transported in a bucket or container that previously contained chemicals, or gasoline, or some other contaminant. Then, once the unsanitary container is filled with water, the people have to carry it to their homes. It is usually the women in Haiti who are retrieving the water, and they usually carry the heavy buckets on their heads.

We have drilled one well that has a manual pump near The Hope Center. It can be accessed 24 hours a day, and many people come daily for their family's water supply. The location of this well has shortened the walking distance for many of those who come each day from nearby villages. In addition, we have a well with an electric pump that provides water for The Hope Center. There is also a well at the orphanage.

EDUCATION

Like clean water, education is necessary for a healthy, successful life. Those with little or no education are doomed to a lifetime of ignorance, darkness, and extreme poverty.

One day I was walking through a nearby village and noticed many children in the local elementary school. As I continued walking I noticed there were quite a few children who were old enough to attend school but were not at school that day. I asked the leader of the school why those children were not in school. He said, "They cannot afford to go to school."

I asked him, "How much does it cost to attend your school?"

He said, "Twenty-five dollars. A year."

I was shocked. Those children were playing in the dirt rather than learning to read and write and do math. They were not learning about science or geography. At their young ages, their fates were sealed. All for $25.

Now, $25 was only for the tuition. It didn't cover a uniform or school supplies or a daily meal while at school. But at that time, those children could be admitted to school for only $25 per school year. We quickly got the word out and American Christians began to sponsor children for school. Before we knew it, over 200 children had been sponsored.

Why do the children have to pay to attend school? The reason is because the government of Haiti cannot afford to put schools in all the towns and villages scattered throughout the country. In most cases, especially in the rural areas, the schools are privately run by the local villagers. They have to acquire a building and hire teachers for their schools. It is part of the culture that the children wear uniforms, or they cannot attend school. If a meal is provided at lunch time, either the school has to raise the funds, or the children have to pay for it through their tuition. With most families having little income and multiple children, it's easy to see how the enormous benefits of an education are out of reach for many children.

As of July 2019, we were sponsoring over 900 children in nearby schools and our own schools. Each child is sponsored for $37 per month. The sponsorships provide tuition, a daily meal, a uniform, and books. This is one of the most effective programs we have and impacts not only the children, but also dozens and dozens of teachers, assistants, cooks, and security guards who receive jobs. Also, the mothers of the children are almost always the ones who prepare the meals. The meal at school each day is one less meal for these poverty-stricken moms to worry about.

Also, with an education the children at least have a chance. Even in Haiti, the ability to read and write, do math, and solve problems gives you a fighting chance. When opportunities arise, these children will be prepared to take advantage of those opportunities.

Around 2014, we realized that most schools in our village of Galette Chambon ended with the 6th grade. Children either dropped out of school or somehow managed to enroll in a secondary school in another village or town. Most of the children of Galette Chambon could not afford to go to school in another place. Thus, many of them ended their educations after the 6th grade. Because of this awful reality, we started a secondary school. Each year we have added an additional grade.

Then, in the spring of 2019 and with the leadership of our missionary Mickie West, we decided it was time to build our own elementary school. We had no funding for this $80,000 project. However, Mickie contacted churches and groups that were planning to take a mission trip to Galette Chambon that summer and asked if they would make the building of a classroom their project for the trip. Most of them agreed, and within weeks we had the funds to build the school. The school was opened in September of 2019. But God!

HIGHER EDUCATION

As I have noted, we believe very strongly in education. We believe every person should receive at least a high school education. And, in some cases, we have been able to help our Haitian friends receive higher education.

His name is Jorese. When we first started working in Haiti, he operated an elementary school in the village. He spoke broken English and would come to the Hope Center to visit with us. One day Jorese shared his dream of going to medical school. Some of our supporters communicated with him and said they would like to help. Jorese applied to medical school and was admitted. For four years he worked very hard and graduated from medical school. Then, in the fall of 2018 he began his residency in the northern part of the country. Jorese is an outstanding young man with great character and a strong work ethic. It is our hope that he will finish his training and one day come back to work with us.

Then there was June. June worked as a translator for us at our Thoman Hope Center. Her English was excellent, and she had a beautiful smile with an outgoing personality. June shared with our missionaries there, Terry and Kathy Warren, that she wanted to be a nurse. Terry and Kathy paid her tuition expenses for three years. In the summer of 2018, June graduated. She is now working part time for us at our clinic in Thoman. We also use her as a translator when we need extra help. This is good for us and gives her additional work until she can work as a nurse full-time.

There was also Wesley. Wesley is the oldest child of Pastor Mathurin in Thoman. He is very smart and speaks good English. As he was growing up, we had several dental teams go to his village and conduct dental clinics. Wesley observed and helped. He took a strong interest in the dental work. Wesley decided he wanted to become a dentist and then return to Thoman and set up a dental clinic at the Hope Center. Wesley graduated from high school and then thought about continuing his education in the United States.

As we thought about it, we realized the best place for Wesley would be with people he knew. Our original missionaries in Thoman, Terry and Kathy Warren, had moved back to northwest Arkansas. There is a community college where they live. Wesley was able to take the ACT test in Haiti. He scored high enough to get into the community college in Northwest Arkansas. So, in December 2016, Wesley moved to Arkansas and enrolled at Northwest Arkansas Community College. For two years, Wesley studied and worked hard. He made all A's his entire two years and graduated with his Associate degree in December 2018. Many BGM supporters helped to pay Wesley's tuition and expenses. Otherwise, he would not have been able to attend.

Thereafter, he moved to Hattiesburg, Mississippi to attend school at William Carey University. Melanie Blanton and her family invited Wesley into their home to live while he attends William Carey. Melanie has been to Haiti countless times and knows Pastor Mathurin and Wesley's family well. No doubt, this will involve major time and financial commitments on the part of Melanie and her husband and three sons. But, they have chosen to invest in Wesley and his future.

Miguelson Charles is a remarkable young Haitian man who began working with a group of Christians in Pensacola, Florida immediately after the earthquake. He wanted to go to law school. Two families from Pensacola helped pay Miguelson's tuition and expenses. Then, once the Pensacola group began working with us to establish an orphanage at our place, Miguelson came to work for us at BGM. He is our go-to guy in Port-au-Prince. He helps with anything we are doing in the city, including getting containers we have shipped through the port in Saint-Marc, Haiti.

Miguelson is a remarkable young man. I've never met anyone quite like him. The extent of his contacts is remarkable. He knows people in low places and in high places. Whenever we have needed something, he simply makes a phone call and gets it done.

Miguelson meets most of our teams at the airport. He goes into the airport, greets them, and leads them out. He helps them get through any challenges with customs. In the early years of our work, we had our own buses in which we would transport our teams. However, because of the roads in Haiti, our buses were constantly breaking down. We were spending a fortune on bus maintenance as well as endless hours and a huge amount of frustration. We finally decided to get out of the bus business.

About that time, Miguelson invested in a couple of large vans. Now, he picks our teams up in his vans and drives them to our Hope Centers. At the end of the week, he picks them up and takes them to the airport. We never have to worry about drivers or fuel for the vans or maintenance issues. His vans are always there and always on time.

In 2018, Miguelson graduated from law school in Haiti. In August of 2019, he will start school at the University of Hawaii law school in Hawaii. He will be working on a Masters degree that will take him two semesters to complete. Our hope is that Miguelson will one day become a great leader in Haiti and lead his country to new heights.

ROOFS

Our work at But God Ministries began with the idea of providing housing for those still living in tent cities. If you ever have the opportunity to visit a tent city, you will see the filth and squalor and hopelessness in which so many people still live years after the earthquake. In fact, the tent city from which we have gotten all of our residents still had over 30,000 people three years after the earthquake. Three years is a long time to live in a one room tent with a piece of tin for a door. The floors are dirt and when it rains they become a mud pit.

In 2013 I was walking through the tent city in the community of Delmas which is located in the heart of Port-au-Prince. Prior to the earthquake, this area was empty and was covered with grass. From 2010-2013, every inch was filled with tents and people and heartache and hopelessness. While walking through the tent city with one of our American teams, I asked a lady if we could look inside her tent. She graciously agreed. We walked inside to find a room about 10 feet by 8 feet. There were a few pots and pans in the corner but not much else. I asked the lady how long she had lived there. She said three years, ever since the earthquake. I then asked her how many people lived in the tent. She said seven. Seven people living in a space that is 10 feet by 8 feet. For three years.

Many people have asked me how we decided who got to move into our houses. We had certain criteria that had to be met and a contract that had to be signed before a family could move into one of our houses. The families had to:

1. Be currently living in a tent because they lost their house in the earthquake
2. Grow a garden after moving into our community
3. Have a job or agree to train for a job
4. Understand they will not own their house for 3 years
5. Get along with other families living in the community
6. Refrain from engaging in behavior that is detrimental to the community or be forced to leave and give up their house; But God Ministries reserves the right to determine which behavior is detrimental to the community

For each family that moved into our houses, we would:

1. Move them in our truck from the tent city to our community
2. Provide one month's supply of rice, beans, and cooking oil
3. Provide one bed and one mattress
4. Provide access to clean water
5. Provide access to health care
6. Provide access to a local church
7. Hook each house to an electric line, but each family is responsible for its own electric bill

There was a four step process for moving into our houses. The first step involved a family being identified as a potential member of our community. We had a trustworthy Haitian man who helped us identify families who would be a good fit for our community.

The second step involved me interviewing the potential families in a room at the tent city in Delmas. During the meeting, I shared the criteria and expectations for all families who moved into our community, and they had the opportunity to ask questions.

The third step included a trip to our community by one of the members of a potential family. During this trip they got to see the houses, the community, and the location of our work. We met in The Hope Center for further questions and answers.

The fourth step included the move from the tent city to our community in our truck.

One of my favorite parts of our work at that time was moving the families into their new homes. In August of 2012 we moved the first 12 families. As we arrived at the tent city with our truck, the families had gathered all their belongings outside their tents. Those belongings were so few in number we were able to move two families and everything they owned plus all the members of the families in one regular sized pick-up truck. Can you imagine? Everything you own plus your family members fitting in one half of the back of a pick-up. One lady had everything she owned sitting on part of a white folding table outside her tent. Everything.

As we walked through the tent city that August to begin moving the first 12 families that had gone through the interview process, an 81 year old Haitian lady grabbed me by the arm. She was tiny. She could not have weighed more than 90 pounds. I was walking that day with the President of our Board of Directors, Buddy Huff. Buddy was a Senior Vice-President for a large, regional bank based in Mississippi. He has a heart the size of Texas and always roots for the underdog.

The lady who grabbed me was named Marta. Through the interpreter who was with me (Haitians speak Creole), she invited us into her tent. We stepped into the first part of her tent. It was small and dark and crowded. But then we noticed a second part of the tent and saw there was light coming through the top. There was a gaping hole in her tent. We asked about the hole and she told us that whenever it rains, her bed gets wet, her other belongings are soaked, and the floor becomes wet and muddy.

After seeing her dire situation, Buddy said to me, "We're going to take her with us today."

I said, "Buddy, I would love to take her but she's not on the list for today. Plus, we have nowhere to put her. There is not a house available for her. But I tell you what we can do. We'll put her at the top of the list for the next set of houses."

Five months later I was back in the tent city moving the next six families from their tents into our houses. One of the first people we got that day was Marta. We loaded her meager belongings onto our truck and headed out of town towards our community. As soon as I could, I picked up my phone and placed a call to Buddy who was in the States. I said, "Good morning, Buddy."

He said, "I know you're in Haiti. How's your day going?"

I said, "It's going great. I'm riding in our truck in Port-au-Prince. Guess who's riding with me."

He asked, "Who?"

I said, "Marta! Our 81 year old friend from the tent city!" Buddy was thrilled beyond words. And so was I, and so was Marta!

About an hour later we arrived at our new community. I helped Marta carry some of her belongings to her new house. On the porch of her house, I handed her the keys and told her to open the door. She put the key in the lock, turned the knob, and stepped into her new home. As she did, Marta threw her hands into the air and began exclaiming, "Praise Jezi! Praise Jezi!" It was a thrilling moment as she praised Jesus for her new home.

While we have marvelous stories of families moving from

the tent cities into our houses, there are so many more who need to move. Once, I was at The Hope Center and it was Family Night. Many of our new residents were there and one of them, Macquil, asked if he could speak to me. We stepped away from the rest of the group. He told me about his cousin, a Haitian lady who has 5 children, and her husband is rarely around. She and the children lived in the tent city in Delmas. Macquil asked if his cousin and her children could have a house. He said their tent has many holes and when it rains their few belongings get wet. The floor of their tent turns into a big mud puddle and they try to scoop out the water and the mud.

Later that night it started raining. Hard. And for a long time. I thought about Macquil's cousin. I thought about the hopelessness and desperation she must have been feeling. I wondered how wet her children's clothes were getting. I wondered if she had a bed and if it was getting wet. I wondered how muddy the floor of their tent was getting. I wondered if they were just miserable. I wondered if we all gave a little more if we could let them know how much God loves them and that He hasn't forgotten about them. I wondered about a lot of things that night. I wondered if I was in the position of Macquil's cousin, through no fault of my own, if anyone would care. I wondered if wealthy people, wealthy Christian people, who have everything they could ever want, plus a little more, would care enough to help my children and me. That night I wondered if I were more faithful and more sacrificial and more focused and more giving if more people's lives could be changed. I wondered.

ECONOMIC DEVELOPMENT

We have come to realize that if we are not creating jobs and providing job training, then we are left with providing only one thing – a handout. And we are not interested in handouts. As I shared earlier in this book, handouts are not good for

Americans, and they're not good for Haitians. It is not our desire to create a sense of dependency on us or to continue a sense of dependency on the government or any non-profit organization. Jobs are the key to sustainability. Jobs, jobs, jobs. I cannot overemphasize the importance of jobs.

Not only do jobs provide economic stability for a person, but jobs also provide dignity and respect. One day we were about to fire one of our security guards. As he pleaded for his job he said, "You have no idea how much respect I receive from my family because I have a job that pays every month." Jobs matter. And the security guard got to keep his!

Economic development, specifically job training and job creation, is one of the most challenging parts of working in a developing country. There are many organizations, like ours, that provide medical care, housing, Bible studies, church plants, orphanages, water wells, and food. But it seems that very few of us do a great job with economic development. This is not only a problem in the developing countries, but also a problem in our churches back home. We offer opportunities for many of our church members to participate: doctors, nurses and other medical personnel, construction workers, Bible study leaders, and people who work with children. Yet countless business men and women are sitting in our pews with no opportunities to uses their skill set. They can go and help build a house, teach a Bible lesson, or help with the logistics of a clinic, but they usually are not afforded the opportunity to do what they do best: help build a successful business.

In the fall of 2012, I was traveling in Port-au-Prince with a new Haitian driver. He was a college student studying accounting. He told me his goal was to graduate and open an accounting firm. As I talked with my American friend about economic development in Haiti, I asked the driver, who spoke very good English, if he wanted Americans to come to Haiti and give him a sandwich. He looked at me with a frown on his face. Before he could say anything, I asked him, "Would it be better for American accountants to come to Haiti and help you set up your accounting firm?"

A huge grin came across his face and he said, "That's the kind of help I need!"

Since we began construction of The Hope Center in May 2011, we have seen economic development and job creation take place in a variety of ways. Over the first eight years of our work in Haiti, we have seen hundreds of jobs created. Some are full-time jobs and some are part-time jobs.

Our full-time jobs include 150 positions: translators, drivers, security guards, cooks, cleaning ladies, orphanage workers, teachers, principals, doctors, nurses, and other medical personnel. Most of our part-time jobs involve construction work. For larger construction projects such as the orphanage and the churches, upwards of 30 men are hired for each building. A smaller number of men are hired for construction of houses and classrooms.

We also have less conventional ways for the Haitians to earn money. In the spring of 2012, I received a call from a lady from Meridian, MS. She said, "Stan, you don't know me but I am going on one of your trips to Haiti in a few weeks. I am going with my church, Highland Baptist Church." She continued, "I have been praying for three years that God would allow me to use my skills to help others in His name but I'm not sure how to go about it."

I said, "What do you do?" She replied, "I am an artist. I paint."

I told her, "Here's what you can do. When you go to Haiti in a few weeks, I will have six Haitian ladies meet you in The Hope Center every morning from 9:00 to 11:00 and you can teach them how to paint. At the same time, we will have six other Haitian ladies meeting with another American. Those ladies will be learning how to make things out of clay such as crosses and nativity sets and Christmas tree ornaments."

She said, "That sounds great. I'll bring all the painting

supplies to get us started." That lady from Meridian then decided to raise the funds for the painting supplies she would need in Haiti. She decided to hold a class at her church on a Saturday and teach women how to paint. She decided to charge each lady $30 for the lesson and all proceeds would go to purchase the painting supplies for Haiti. She thought she might have ten or twelve ladies sign up for her class, but she was wrong. Fifty women from her church signed up to take painting lessons! She raised $1,500 to help the ladies of Haiti begin a painting business.

The first morning of her trip to Haiti, six Haitian ladies showed up for painting lessons. By the end of the week, they had learned to paint. At the same time, six other Haitian ladies were learning to make objects from the clay. At the end of the week, these ladies sold their creations to the American team members who were visiting The Hope Center that week. Now, at the end of each week when we have a team in Haiti, the ladies set up a table with their goods to sell to our teams. The teams are not compelled to buy anything. However, most team members want to take a souvenir home with them. They want the souvenir to be native to Haiti, and there is nowhere else for them to buy souvenirs. So, we have a product, and we have a real, legitimate, market. These ladies have made up to $100 per month through selling their creations, and this is a significant amount for an uneducated Haitian woman to add to her family's income. It should be noted that since we are trying to teach business principles, we make the ladies purchase the clay from us in order to create more items to sell. We want them to understand they must save some of their profits to reinvest in their business.

One of the larger and more successful economic development successes we have had involves a Haitian general contractor named Jacques. Initially, we contracted with an American non-profit called Thirst No More that was building houses in Haiti. Craig Miller was the President of Thirst

No More, and Jacques was an employee. He worked as their construction supervisor in Haiti. Jacques, as an employee of Thirst No More, was responsible for building The Hope Center, the orphanage, and our first 23 houses. Then, Thirst No More made the decision to focus on their work in Africa and cease their work in Haiti. Their goal all along had been to set Jacques up with his own construction company whenever they left the country. So today, Jacques has his own construction company and has built two churches, a second missionary house, 100 more houses, numerous classrooms, and a second Hope Center that contains missionary housing, dorms for visiting teams, a large kitchen, and a medical-dental clinic.

I am thrilled with our relationship with Jacques. We now have a Haitian man, owning a Haitian company, hiring Haitian employees, purchasing Haitian materials, and building Haitian buildings in Haitian communities. Assuming both of us are happy with the relationship, we have enough work to keep Jacques busy for a long time. Plus, he is free to take on more work as his business grows. This is truly economic development. But God!

Following the development of the relationship with Jacques, we helped another Haitian man, Jonel, start a construction company in the village of Thoman. Jonel has built a brand new elementary school, numerous classrooms at the original school in Thoman, and many houses. Like Jacques, he is a Haitian man who hires Haitian employees and builds Haitian buildings for Haitian people.

Another business enterprise developed the first week we started construction on The Hope Center in May 2010. The second day we were there, I noticed two ladies appeared about 30 feet from where we were building. They put up four sticks and pulled a tarp over the sticks for shade. Then they brought a cooler full of drinks - ice cold drinks. We were hot and sweaty and thirsty. So we began buying drinks from them. Shortly thereafter, they began cooking meals for lunch and selling them in Styrofoam plates. I cannot tell you how impressed I was with these ladies. This was free enterprise at its best. I thought they should have received the Entrepreneur of the Year Award. They saw a need, moved to fill that need, and created a business in the process.

Another business we have helped develop is a sewing business in the village of Galette Chambon. All of the schools in Haiti require the students to wear uniforms. We set up tow ladies and a young man with their own sewing company. They makes hundreds of uniforms each year for numerous schools.

SOIL

Access to healthy food is an important factor in community development. In Haiti, many people live without access to healthy food. While we are not a give-away organization, we do make food distributions during times of drought or other crisis. We simply will not allow people to starve when we have the means to provide food.

In addition, we have provided a well and pipes to irrigate 75 acres of farmland in Galette Chambon, Haiti.

I WAS THINKING . . .

Do something. DO something. DO SOMETHING. Get up, get going, and do something. Oh, not for you. Or me. Do something for children who are hungry, families who are living in tents, women who cannot read or write, men who have no jobs to support their families. Do something. With what, you ask? With your time and your talent and your treasure. Do something with you. Your person. Your self. You. After all, you have much to offer.

Stop protesting. I know you don't speak multiple languages, and you haven't mastered every aspect of Christian theology, and you've never conducted surgery in a jungle. But you have a heart for the poor. You really do want to help the suffering. You want to see lives changed. So do something.

You have time. Just as much as everyone else. Those two hours of television watching each day amount to 14 hours each week that could be used for greater purposes. Use that time to volunteer, to invest in hurting people, to think and plan and research and organize. Use that time to make a difference. All that internet surfing is helping no one. So spend your time on something that matters and that shares God's love with a desperate, hurting world.

You have abilities. Yes, you do. Your abilities would include your education, work skills, family background, life experiences, and relationships. Also, that get-it-done attitude. What could you do? Well, what do you want to do? Where are your interests? Explore those and see how God has wired you and then use those interests as a road map to service.

You have treasure. The truth is that if you make $50,000 per year your income is higher than 99% of the people of the world. Congratulations! You're wealthy, and you didn't even know it. So give. A lot. Spend less on self and more on others. It will be a lot more rewarding than buying yet another gadget for yourself or your family. In fact, give so much that it hurts.

Give so much that it's a sacrifice. That you are unable to buy something else or do something else because you are giving so much for the glory of God and the benefit of others. Can we honestly say with King David, "I will not sacrifice to the Lord my God burnt offerings that cost me nothing" (2 Samuel 24:24).

So, what's the hold-up? Get going. There are hungry people who need food. Sick people who need medicine. Lonely people who need a friend. Hurting people who need comfort. Homeless people who need shelter. Lost people who need Jesus. And God has a plan. That plan is YOU! That plan is ME! Have fun and DO SOMETHING!!

CHAPTER 9

New Partner

He was the pastor of his church in the remote mountain village of Thoman, located about an hour and a half drive from our first community in Galette Chambon. Every week, Pastor Mathurin worked for us as we built a brand new community. He never asked for anything for himself or his village of Thoman. He just faithfully worked for us as we built the community in Galette Chambon.

When he first began working for us in the spring of 2011, Pastor Mathurin spoke very little English. But, he was wise enough to know that if he really wanted to partner with BGM, he needed to learn English so that he could communicate better with us. So, unbeknownst to us, he signed up for English lessons. Little by little his English improved. Finally, one day as he and I were going to Port-au-Prince to run some errands, I realized we did not need to take an interpreter with us. His English had gotten so good that he and I could communicate really well. That was a turning point in his work for BGM and in our relationship.

Pastor Mathurin lived with his wife, seven children, and two nephews, in a very small two room structure in Thoman. Often, the children would sleep in nearby structures on a concrete floor. I thought that was not a good situation, and that if we were ever going to do more work in the village of Thoman, Pastor

Mathurin would need more appropriate housing for his family. So, in November of 2013 we designed a three bedroom house with a bathroom, kitchen, and dining area. Of course, we had no funds to pay for the house, but at least we had a drawing.

A few weeks after we designed the house, I was teaching my Lifegroup class at Broadmoor Baptist Church in Madison, MS. It was near Christmas and I told the class about a rule we have in our family. The rule is that every year at Christmas no one in our family receives a gift that is of greater value that what we give to Jesus. After all, Christmas is the celebration of a birthday. If we were to give greater gifts to ourselves, it would be like me showing up at your birthday party and saying, "You should see the expensive gift I bought myself for your birthday. It's really great!" That would be foolish. It would make no sense. Yet that's exactly what many of us do every year at Christmas.

I told the class that a gift to Jesus could take many forms. I then told them my family was donating money to help build a house for Pastor Mathurin and his family in Haiti. I described how he worked very hard helping us build a community that was not his own and that he never complained and never asked for anything for himself. Then I gave other examples of how people could give to our church, to local ministries, or to others who were in need.

After the class, a man and his wife walked directly to me. The man said, "Would $20,000 help to build the house for the pastor in Haiti?"

I said, "As a matter of fact, it would!" He said that a check would be delivered to my office the next day. To say the least, I was very excited. However, I did not know the man very well and therefore didn't know if he would follow through. Much to my delight, the next day a man showed up at our office and delivered a check for $20,000. More funds were raised and shortly thereafter we began construction on the new house. Pastor Mathurin and his family have been living in the house ever since.

In the first few months of 2013, Pastor Mathurin decided to apply for a visa from the U.S. embassy in Haiti so that he could travel to the United States. Fortunately, he was approved for a five year visa and we began planning his first trip to the States. We decided that on his first trip to the U. S. he would travel with me and stay in my home. His trip would last from April 5 to April 20.

The day before we were leaving Haiti for the States, I sat down with Pastor Mathurin. I said to him, "I need to tell you something. I live in a big house, a really big house."

He said, "I thought you did."

And then I said to him, "All the other Americans you have met over the last couple of years also live in big houses. I want you to be prepared for that."

The next day we boarded a plane and flew from Port-au-Prince to Ft. Lauderdale. It was his first time on a plane. From Ft. Lauderdale we flew to Dallas where we had to ride the tram from one concourse to another. When the tram came, the door opened and we stepped inside. Then the tram took off. Pastor Mathurin looked around and asked, "Where is the conductor?"

I said, "There is no conductor. A computer runs it."

He said, "No, really. Where is the conductor?" I told him again that there was no conductor and that it was run by a computer. When we arrived at the next concourse, the tram door and the door to the building opened at exactly the same time. He marveled, "They opened perfectly."

I said, "Every time."

We finally made it from Dallas to Jackson and a board member, Barbara Gladney, and her husband, Bob, picked us up at the airport. It was about 9:00 p.m. As we got near our house I asked Bob, who was driving, to go through the Chick-fil-A drive-thru so we could grab something to eat. Later, Pastor Mathurin would say, "Bob pulled up to the box and said, 'I want two number 1's and two lemonades. Then we drove around the building and they handed us the food. It was a miracle!"

Why did he think it was a miracle? Because in his remote village in the mountains, if you want something to eat, then a fire must be started and the cooking process can take hours. And yet we received cooked food in less than two minutes. It is pretty miraculous!

The next morning, I took Pastor Mathurin with me to run several errands. First, I went to get a haircut. He went inside and waited while my hair was cut. Afterwards, we walked outside and got into my car. He looked at me and said, "A woman cut your hair!" That was one of many things that would be new for him.

We then went to a brand new Kroger grocery store. It is the largest one in the state of Mississippi. It's huge. There were aisles and aisles of food. All kinds of food. Of course, there is not one grocery store in his village of Thoman.

We left the grocery store, and I stopped by a bank and used the ATM machine. Pastor Mathurin later described it this way: "Pastor Stan drove up to the bank. He rolled down the window and put a card into the machine. Then it gave him some money!" This was another shocking experience.

One place I wanted him to see was the church where all of our work in Haiti started – First Baptist Church of Jackson, MS (FBCJ). I knew this would be another shocking experience. After all, his church in Thoman was a concrete block structure about 45 feet long and 20 feet wide. It had a roof of rusted tin being held up with tree limbs for trusses. The people sat on old benches with no backs. On the other hand, the sanctuary at FBCJ is a magnificent structure that seats 3,000 people, is made of beautiful dark wood, and has an organ with 10,000 pipes. The contrast could not be any greater. And, while his church facility consists of only the small sanctuary, FBCJ has over 700,000 square feet of space including Sunday School rooms, offices, a double gymnasium with walking track and racquet ball court, two fellowship halls, the largest kitchen in downtown Jackson, and a Counseling Center. How would I explain all of this to him?

Later that week I took him to Broadmoor Baptist Church, the church my family joined after leaving FBCJ. This was another surprising experience for him. Unlike the FBCJ sanctuary, the Broadmoor worship center is a more modern looking facility with 2,500 theater seats. Once again, this was in sharp contrast to the church in Thoman, Haiti where Pastor Mathurin serves as pastor.

Many people who had been to Haiti and who knew Pastor Mathurin wanted to visit with him. One group took him bowling! I assure you there are no bowling alleys in his village. He caught on quickly and scored 77 on his first game!

One Sunday morning, he and I were driving to a church to speak. It was quiet in the car. He had been in the States for over a week. I knew it could all be overwhelming so I said to him, "You've been here a week, and you've seen a lot. Are you OK?"

He said, "Now I understand how much Americans sacrifice to come to Haiti." I was astounded. I couldn't believe what he had just said.

I quickly responded, "Pastor, thank you for saying that. However, don't worry about the Americans. They're fine. They're just fine." It shocked me that he was thinking of the Americans. We Americans have every material blessing known to mankind. We live lives that many of the world cannot even imagine. The idea that we are sacrificing ourselves into poverty is laughable. I was grateful that he was thinking of us Americans, but I assured him that the Americans are doing well, and we actually could give a great deal more.

Since that visit in 2013, Pastor Mathurin has made many more visits to the States. He has been to Virginia, Washington D.C., and Arkansas. He travels to the States numerous times each year to visit friends, take some vacation time, and speak with our partner churches. He is a seasoned traveler, his English is really good, and he needs no help getting around.

On one visit a few years after his initial trip, he brought his wife with him. Her name is Genese and she gives leadership to their school in addition to running their household. Her trip to the States was even more shocking than her husband's. He had spent some time in Port-au-Prince before going to America, but most of her time had been spent in their remote mountain village. I flew with them. One morning she and Pastor Mathurin walked around my house and saw my neighbor's house. She wanted to know which church that was. I was embarrassed to explain that it wasn't a church. It was a house, and only two people lived there.

The next day I could not find them in our house and looked out the window to see them walking on the sidewalk down the street. I immediately went to check on them. When I walked up to them, she was looking around and saying something to Pastor Mathurin. Because she does not speak English, and I do not speak Haitian Creole, I asked Pastor Mathurin what she was saying. He replied that she said there was no way she could explain this to the people in her village. She's right, of course. How do you explain houses with thousands of square feet to people who live in mud huts? How do you explain the streets and the sidewalks and the lampposts? How do you explain that most families not only have a car, but a car for every person in the family?

One Sunday while Pastor Mathurin and Genese were staying with us, we drove a couple of hours to Jonestown, Mississippi where BGM had started working in the Mississippi Delta. That morning I was preaching at St. Luke's Missionary Baptist Church, which is 100% African-American. During the service, I introduced several people who were visiting with us. I then told them that we had special guests all the way from the country of Haiti. I asked Pastor Mathurin to come to the platform to say a few words. I wasn't sure what he would say. Pastor Mathurin looked over the crowd and said, "I want to

say hello to all my cousins. You look like my grandparents!"
Everyone laughed and we had a great time of worship that day.

After the service, we drove to Oxford, Mississippi about an hour away. I wanted them to go to the campus of Ole Miss and see an American university. My daughter was a student at that time living in the Kappa Delta sorority house. This was yet another surprising experience as they saw how American college students are able to live.

I WAS THINKING . . .

"What's the point? You can't help 'em all."

"That's just a drop in the bucket."

"There are just too many of them."

We've all heard these lovely words. We've even thought the same things. We try to live out the commands of God in relation to others but the problems, the obstacles, the sheer number of people, are overwhelming. So, what's the answer? If we can't minister to everyone, we should minister to no one?

Then I think about what he did. He helped individuals. Not just nameless, faceless, abstract creatures. No. Real people. With real families and real problems and real hurts. Like the paralyzed guy whose friends lowered him through the roof directly to the feet of Jesus. That guy had a name. He had a mom and a dad. He had friends. Good ones. He had dreams and desires and hopes. And he got healed. Him. Personally. He got up and walked and ran and talked and rejoiced with his family. His life was made infinitely better. His life. And it mattered.

This Jesus seemed to care for the individual. For men and women and boys and girls. For sinners, like that short guy who climbed up a tree (really???) and ended up hosting Jesus for dinner. Jesus went to his house. Sat at his table. Ate his food. And called the religious hypocrites who questioned his actions idiots. Ok. So that didn't happen. Just wishful thinking on my part. But the rest is true.

And then there was that time he told those stories about the lost sheep. Just one of 99 was missing. And the lost coin. Just one of 10 was missing. And the people in the stories looked for the one sheep and the one coin. And this Jesus guy said that God feels the same way about lost people. In fact, God is so stoked about lost people being found that Jesus said, "I tell you, there is rejoicing in the presence of the angels of God over one sinner who repents."[5]

So this is really good news. We don't have to help them all. We don't have to minister to every last one of them. Just the ones God puts in front of us. Help one here and help another there. And what's neat is that if I help some, and you help some, and the other one billion Christians help some, then there would be a lot of people being helped. A lot of love being shared.

And one other thing, if you don't have much influence or much money or much of anything, this helping others deal is just for you. You can take your little influence and your little money and help one little person. In His name. And then, watch how He blesses your efforts in ways you never dreamed possible. Watch how He takes your little and makes much. Watch how He takes your love and your care and your out-stretched arms and multiplies it all in such a way that you know it was Him, He gets all the glory, and you get all the satisfaction. Happy helping!

---

[5] Luke 15:10 – NIV translation

Stan Buckley

CHAPTER 10

Expansion

When we started our work in Haiti in 2011, our plans did not include a second location. We were committed to building one community in Galette Chambon. However, for three years beginning in 2012, we would take mission teams that were staying in Galette Chambon to Pastor Mathurin's village of Thoman each Sunday. The teams would drive up the mountain to Thoman, attend the worship service, eat lunch, walk around the village, and then return to Galetter Chambon for the rest of the week.

One day in early 2013 I said to Pastor Mathurin, "I have a dream that one day God is going to allow us to build a Hope Center in Thoman. I have no idea how that can happen, but I believe it will."

Pastor Mathurin looked at me and said, "I have the same dream."

In March 2013, believing that God would turn this dream into reality, I stood to greet the congregation in Thoman and to do my usual duty of introducing the American mission team that was with me. While standing before the church, I made an important announcement. I announced that the following year (2014) we would begin construction on a Hope Center that would include a medical-dental clinic in their village. The response was loud and immediate. The people were thrilled because there is no medical care there. There is no electricity and no running water. There are very few jobs.

At that time, I had no idea how we would pull this off. I had no idea where the money would come from or how we would get all the building materials to Thoman to build an enormous walled compound. But I did know that God Himself had given us a vision for that community and that He was more than capable of providing the means to build a new Hope Center.

Then God went to work – again! It was about that time that Jim Gorrie had gone on a mission trip to Galette Chambon. After the trip, Jim called me and said, "I'm an Auburn University guy. The schools of nursing and architecture and building science at Auburn have been working in Ecuador the past five years. Those projects recently ended. I was wondering if I called a meeting at my office in Birmingham for Auburn professors and for churches that our company built in the Birmingham area, would you come share your story?" I told him I thought I could work that out. Shortly thereafter, I found myself in a large meeting room in Birmingham with dozens of professors and pastors. I shared what God had been doing through BGM.

Several months later, I found myself in Thoman, Haiti with 9 Auburn professors on a site for a new Hope Center. Those professors measured and studied and took notes. Then, they went back to Auburn and Scott Kramer, one of the professors from the Auburn University College of Architecture, Design, and Construction, asked his top two students in the Building Science program to design a new Hope Center in Thoman. The top two students that year happened to be female and they needed a project for their senior thesis. Our new Hope Center became their project. From August to December of 2013, those students designed the new Hope Center.

In early 2014, we took the designs for the new Hope Center and raised $140,000 with 4 of our committed donors. They each gave $35,000. Then, one of our Board members, Mark Rich, went to Thoman and made video interviews of the local residents and of Pastor Mathurin. Mark did a super job of showing the needs of Thoman. He then designed a beautiful brochure, and we included a DVD of his interviews in each brochure. We then mailed the brochures to our donor base and asked them to match the $140,000 that had already been given so that we could raise $280,000 to build the new Hope Center. Within a couple of months, our faithful donors had matched the $140,000, and we had the funds in place to build the new Hope Center. But God!

In May of 2014, we started construction on the new Hope Center. It took approximately 8 months to complete. Our Haitian contractor, Jacques Joseph, did an amazing job under difficult circumstances. All of the building materials – sand, water, concrete, cement blocks – had to be brought up the mountain to the job site. Many people received jobs during those eight months. In January of 2015, our missionaries moved into the Hope Center and began ministering through that structure.

The Hope Center was built on a slight incline and is divided into three distinct areas. The top section is the private area. It contains our missionary house as well as dorms and bathroom for our visiting mission teams, enabling us to host 32 people on a mission trip. The middle section is our semi-private area. It contains a large kitchen, laundry area, office, and a covered meeting/eating area. The bottom section contains our medical-dental clinic and a covered waiting area for patients.

What I really like about the Hope Center is the fact that while it enables us to provide medical care for the people of Thoman, it is much more than a clinic. From the new Hope Center, we partner with the Haitian people to provide: new housing (70 as of February 2019), jobs, increased educational opportunities for the children (over 400 children sponsored at local schools), clean water, and the Good News of the gospel.

We held the Dedication Ceremony for the newly completed Hope Center in November of 2014. It was a glorious day of celebration. A robed choir walked in single file from the local church, down the street, and into the Hope Center. Our missionaries and staff from our original Hope Center in Galette Chambon were there. Scott Kramer, the Auburn professor from the Building Science department was there. Without Scott, we could never have built the Hope Center as we did. Jim Gorrie, President of Brasfield & Gorrie Construction Company, was there. He had introduced us to Scott and provided great encouragement and support, including sending teams to help with the construction. Billy Van Devender, one of our BGM Board members, was there. Jacques Joseph, the Haitian contractor who built the facility, was there. Mike and Jann Kenney, along with Patton Ford, were present. They had been responsible for the plumbing work. And dozens of local citizens were there. It was day I will never forget as we sang hymns, read Scripture, and praised God for His blessings.

In May of 2016, electrical engineering students from Georgia Tech did the unthinkable. They made the entire Thoman Hope Center solar powered! This was a huge deal since we were using a generator to provide electricity. I have often said that whenever I hear the generator running, it sounds to me like the sound of money burning. Fuel is expensive in Haiti!

Frank Lambert was a research professor at Georgia Tech. Several years earlier he had begun going to Haiti with his church from Palmetto, Georgia. Frank decided to get his university involved in our work. This first step was to assemble a team of Masters and Ph.D. level students who were interested in the project. The two student leaders were Szilard from Hungary and Felipe from Chile. They worked over a year planning the project, including making multiple trips to the Hope Center in Thoman.

After much preparation and raising over $60,000 for supplies, the students shipped over 30 solar panels, 16 batteries weighing 400 lbs. each, plus wiring, computers, panels, and other supplies. Then, an incredibly diverse group of students from all over the world descended upon the Hope Center and installed a solar powered energy system in a mere 4 days. The students were from all over the U.S. plus China, India, Ethiopia, Hungary, Chile, and even Haiti. The system they installed has worked beautifully. Because we don't have AC units in Thoman, almost everything we have is powered with this system – lights, fans, refrigerators, computers. In addition, we have saved a fortune in fuel costs.

MEDICAL CLINIC

One of the first things we did was open the medical clinic at the new Hope Center in Thoman. Of course, we needed a Haitian doctor, but where would we find a doctor who was familiar with Thoman and who was willing to work in that remote mountain village?

Of course, God knew! As we began looking for a Haitian doctor, Pastor Mathurin told me about a man who had grown up in Thoman. This man's father sent him to medical school across the border in the Dominican Republic. At that time, the man was working in a clinic in Port-au-Prince. His name is Dr. Julot.

Pastor Mathurin contacted Dr. Julot to see if he would be interested in coming back to his home village to provide medical care. He said yes! We interviewed him, and he started serving as the physician in our clinic in 2015. He has done a great job and sees patients from Thoman as well as countless people from villages high in the mountains.

NEW SCHOOL

Mathias is a beautiful and remote village beyond Thoman. You cannot get there by vehicle. It sits on a plateau surrounded by mountains and a cliff that drops to a river bed below. The only way to get there is to walk. When you arrive in Mathias, you feel as though you have stepped back in time hundreds of years. There is no electricity, no running water, no machinery of any sort, and people live in huts made of sticks and dried mud. However, there are people there - wonderful, kind people. Some of the children of Mathias are sponsored though our BGM sponsorship program, and they walk over an hour to school each day. They walk over the mountain and down a long road to Pastor Mathurin's school in Thoman.

In April of 2017, three college girls sent me an email. They had all served as interns at our Thoman Hope Center. They said they believed the village of Mathias needed its own school. They had seen the little children walking to school, and they thought it would be infinitely better if they could go to school in their village. These young ladies – Mati Spencer, Lynsey Hart, and Callie Watson – told me they would do whatever needed to be done to help Mathias get a school.

My initial thoughts after reading their email were not positive. I thought this was yet another project for which I would have to raise money, and all the work would fall on me. I didn't have time for their project. So, I told them I wasn't going to raise any funds, but they were welcome to give it a shot. They asked how much they should raise. I knew they were college students with no jobs and no income, so without doing any research I told them $20,000. I figured that would send them on their way, and I could get back to the projects I was already working on.

These girls were undeterred by my response of $20,000. They immediately developed a website and began raising funds, primarily through social media. Within a few weeks, they had raised over $20,000! That meant I had to get busy planning the construction of a new school in a place where trucks and other vehicles cannot travel.

I contacted our Haitian contractor in Thoman, Jonel, and asked him whether we could get the building materials to Thoman and how much it would cost. These materials included cement blocks, bags of concrete, sand, water, boards, and tin. Jonel told me that he would hire people of the village to carry all the supplies up the mountain, and he gave me a price of

$40,000 to build several classrooms, office space, a kitchen, and restrooms.

Construction began on the school in June of 2017. Prior to construction, the people of the village gathered on the land to pray over their new school. Many people received temporary jobs hauling materials and helping to build the school. In addition, after the construction was completed, we hired one principal, three teachers for the three grades, three assistant teachers, two cooks, and one cleaning lady. All of the salaries and other expenses of the school are funded through our child sponsorship program in which children are sponsored for school at $37 per month.

We opened the school in September of 2017 with the three preschool grades. Each year we have added a grade. As of this writing, we are in our third year of school and have added two grades and two new classrooms. We are very happy for the community. The school has been a wonderful source of pride for the village as they now have their very own school, something many of them never dreamed of having.

HOUSING

House construction is a major emphasis for us in Haiti. By July 2019, we had built approximately 150 houses. Many of those houses were built for families living in deplorable situations. Often times, their houses are mud huts made of sticks, thatch, and dried mud. The roofs may leak, and the floors are made of dirt. Those houses are unsafe and unsanitary.

In January of 2015, a mission team from Oregon was building a house about 300 yards from the main road in Thoman. They took a break and began exploring a nearby area. That's when they stumbled onto one of the worst housing situations we've encountered in Haiti. They found a family living in circumstances in which that most of us would not allow an animal to live. The structure was in the shape of a tent, like a triangle. The floor was dirt, and the sides consisted of rusted tin. The entire structure was about 10 feet long and 7 feet wide. A mother and her four children lived in that structure. They had been living there for years. The mother's name was Mary Minne.

Immediately, the Oregon team alerted Terry and Kathy Warren, our missionaries in Thoman. Kathy emailed me a photo of Mary Minne's living conditions. I knew my lifegroup was going on a mission trip to Haiti in a couple of months, and we had not decided on the main project. On a Saturday night I texted the photo to Rick Adams who was leading the trip. I said, "Rick, if you show this photo in lifegroup tomorrow, I think I know what the project will be." The next day I was preaching at a different church. After preaching, I went back to an office where I had left my keys and my phone. When I picked up the phone I saw a text from Rick.

It said, "I showed the photo to our lifegroup today. We're going to build Mary Minne a new house. And this morning we raised $5,885 to build it!"

Two months later, in March of 2015, 30 of us from my lifegroup at Broadmoor Baptist Church in Madison, MS arrived in Thoman. We started building the new house for Mary Minne. As we worked, Mary Minne said, "You are helping us move from hell to paradise."

During construction, Mary Minne provided bread and coffee for the workers. For the Haitian workers, she cooked rice and beans for lunch. Her oldest daughter, Matride, worked harder than any of the Haitian or American workers.

I visit Mary Minne almost every time I am in Haiti. Today, thanks to the grace of God and the generosity of His people, her family can enter a sturdy and dry home every night. They can lock the door and be safe. They can live with dignity and a sense of hope for the future.

Sometime after we completed the house, another team

built a bed and provided a new mattress for Mary Minne. Then, another team built a table and two benches where they can eat. In addition, because of our holistic approach to ministry, Mary Minne's youngest son was sponsored at the local school where he gets a meal every day; the entire family has access to our medical clinic, and they have a church to attend. But God!

Later that year, in October of 2015, I hosted a mission team in Thoman from Colonial Heights Baptist Church in Ridgeland, MS. I had been serving as Interim Pastor of that church for about a year when we went to Haiti together. Our plans that week included dental work with an oral surgeon who was part of the team, building a house, painting the school, hosting a Ladies Bible study, and providing a food distribution since there had been a drought for many months.

Several months before we left on the mission trip, a man in the church named David approached me and asked how much the houses cost that we build in Haiti. I told him the cost was $5,885. He said he and his wife, Tricia, didn't have that kind of money at the time, so it might take a year or two to save up. I told him that was perfectly fine because there would still be people in Haiti needing houses in one or two years.

The Sunday before we were leaving on our mission trip, David walked up to me and handed me a large manila envelope and then he walked away. I opened the envelope and found a letter, a ledger, and a check for $5,885. The letter explained that David told a friend what he and Tricia were trying to do. The friend was a computer guru and said he would create a website for them and get all kinds of people involved and meet the goal. David went home that night, thought about what his friend had said, and called his friend the next morning. He thanked his friend for the offer but told him they had decided they were going to do it a different way. They decided whatever unexpected funds they received would be God's way of providing the resources for the house. Then, they recorded on the ledger every penny they unexpectedly received. And I mean every penny!

The ledger reported 37 cents found in the church parking lot, 50 cents found at the zoo. David, though retired, mowed several yards and set that money aside. Tricia worked overtime and applied those funds to the goal. Little by little, the money added up. Finally, they were only $2,000 short of the goal.

About that time, their vehicle died. They didn't want to get another one, but they had no choice. They went to a car dealer, agreed on a price, and then went home to think it over until the next day. The next morning they woke up and decided they didn't want to spend that much money on a car. David called the salesman at the dealership. Before David could tell the man they weren't going to buy the car, the man said, "I'm so glad you called. I arrived at work this morning and discovered the car you looked at has been marked down $2,000." David and Tricia bought that car and added the $2,000 savings to the amount already collected for the new house.

Now, back to the trip with Colonial Heights. We arrived safely in Thoman, Haiti, on Saturday. On Sunday we went to church. On Monday morning, part of the team began construction of a house. This house had nothing to do with the house for which David and Tricia had saved. This house was for a man named Vertille, his wife, and their children. Vertille and his family had been living in a hut high in the mountains. They had recently moved to Thoman but had no home of their own.

As we participated in the construction of the house, I noticed an older lady came to the work site each day to pick up rocks and toss them in the pile for the footings. Her name was Ellismene. Initially, I thought she was related to Vertille and would be living in the house. However, I learned that she was a neighbor who was simply volunteering and asked nothing for her labor. Then I was told she was a widow and had no income.

One day while we were taking a break, I asked Ellismene to show me her house. We walked 50 yards from our work site until we came to a miserable little building. We went inside and I saw an old blanket on the concrete. That was Ellismene's bed. I was heartbroken to see these living conditions. And that's when I remembered! That's when I remembered that David and Tricia had given the funds for a new house. I immediately called Pastor Mathurin, told him about the situation, and he confirmed that it would be okay to build a house for Ellismene.

That afternoon, the rest of the mission team came to the construction site. We gathered around Ellismene and, with an interpreter, shared the great news that she would be getting a new house of her own. Upon receiving this news, Ellismene threw her hands into the air and exclaimed in Haitian Creole, "Praise Jezi! Praise Jezie!" Praise Jesus! Praise Jesus!

The next week after our team had returned to the States, our Haitian construction crew built Ellismene's new house. Another team painted it. Then, another team built her a bed and bought her a brand new mattress. No more sleeping on a blanket on the floor. Praise Jezi!

READING, WRITING, AND EATING

In the remote mountain village of Thoman, there is one government school. It can only educate a certain number of children. Because that school is always full, hundreds and hundreds of other children do not have a chance to receive an education.

Pastor Mathurin decided that more children in his village should receive an education. So, he started a school at his house. When I first saw his school in 2012, there were two or three classrooms and two outdoor classrooms. He tried to charge tuition for the children to attend, but most of the people in his village have very little income. As can be imagined, it was difficult to pay for the teachers and all the other expenses that come with operating a school.

About that time, Pastor Mathurin met Terry Warren who would later move to Thoman with his wife, Kathy, as our first missionaries there. Terry is a veteran of the Air Force and had retired from a career in financial planning. He got involved in Haiti following the earthquake in 2010. Kathy is a Registered Nurse.

Terry and Kathy have played a pivotal role in the life of BGM. After visiting Thoman and ministering in that community, they both felt a calling from God to move to Haiti and work in Thoman. In fact, Kathy wrote a poem about her calling, and that poem has been painted onto a wall at the Hope Center in Thoman. It says:

I climbed up a hill my first day in Haiti,
and there she was just standing there waiting.
A dirty, pitiful, sad little girl,
who looked to me like she carried the world.
Her eyes were dark and mesmerizing
as I stared at them I began realizing
the God I love is in this place
I see Him there in the little girl's face.
Right then and there on a hill in Thoman
My heart was broken and my doubt was gone.
God was faithful and answered my prayer
and I knew that He truly did care.
"These are My people, humble and poor,
please love them and feed them and open the door.
Tell them about Me and my undying love.
Tell them I'm watching them from above.
Tell them that Jesus can live in their hearts.
They just have to ask and that is the start
of a life filled with hope, truth, and light,
a life eternal in His sight."
I listened in awe as God called me that day

through the eyes of a child in just the right way
to go with my husband and church family
to love on children in Thoman, Haiti.

Terry told Pastor Mathurin that he sponsored several children in Haiti with Compassion International. He said he would go to their office in Port-au-Prince and talk to them about sponsoring children in Thoman. Pastor Mathurin thought that would be a great idea.

Sometime later, Terry returned from his meeting in Port-au-Prince. He looked dejected. He told Pastor Mathurin that he had bad news. Compassion International had other plans and would not be sponsoring children in Thoman. Then Terry said, "Kathy and I can sponsor some children." Pastor Mathurin asked him, "How many?" Terry said, "Only three." And Pastor Mathurin said, "Then we'll start with three." And so they did.

When Terry returned home to Pea Ridge, Arkansas at the end of the week, he shared with his pastor what had happened. His pastor, Al Fowler, told him to put the church down for 20 more children to be sponsored. Now they had 23!

Terry then started a nonprofit organization called Friends Loving Friends in Christ. The purpose of the organization was to continue the sponsorship program Terry had started. Terry kept telling the story of the sponsorship wherever he went. Before long, they had over 100 children sponsored. Each child was being sponsored for $37 per month. The child received a uniform, tuition, books, supplies, and a meal every day. The meal was extremely important because it might be the only meal the child would eat each day.

In the spring of 2015, we had just opened our new Hope Center in Thoman. I told Terry that we would be sending hundreds of people to Thoman each year and many of them would want to sponsor a child. I believed it would be much easier to transition the sponsorship program to BGM. We had the office staff, accounting measures, and infrastructure to expand the program. Terry and Friend Loving Friends in Christ agreed, and in 2015 BGM took over the child sponsorship program that Terry had so faithfully started.

Terry and Kathy served full time in Thoman during the entire year of 2015. They opened the Hope Center and hosted our first teams. They helped establish the medical clinic. They built houses. They carried on ministry in a remarkable way and helped us get off to a great start in Thoman. At the end of 2015 they moved back to Northwest Arkansas to help care for their grandson. Since that time, they have been to Thoman countless times, hosted many teams, and raised large amounts of money to build houses and complete other projects.

After Terry and Kathy returned to the States, Andrew and Laura Rader moved to Thoman as our missionaries there. They loved the people and did a great job ministering to the locals as well as the mission teams. After two years, they moved back to the States, and since that time we have not had full-time missionaries. Instead, Pastor Mathurin and one of our translators, Kenterson, have given leadership and logistical support for all of our work there.

Since BGM took over the child sponsorship program in 2015, we have seen remarkable growth. We have grown from sponsoring 200 children in 2014 to over 900 children in 2019. I will never forget when my wife and I started sponsoring our first child back in 2015. Terry and I were walking down the dirt road in Thoman. A little girl started walking beside us. It was 10:00 in the morning. I asked Terry, "Why isn't this little girl in school?"

He said, "Her family cannot afford to send her to school."

She had a five gallon bucket in her hand. I asked Terry, "Where is she going?" He said that she was going to walk a mile down the mountain to the river. She was going to fill her bucket with water, and it would weigh about 45 pounds. Then, she was going to put that bucket on her head and walk back up the mountain. She would do it again later in the day.

At that moment, I thought to myself, "As long as God

gives me breath, this little girl will go to school." It was shortly thereafter that my wife and I began sponsoring her for $37 per month. We spend that much when we go out to eat! I set it up on automatic draft from my checking account, and I never have to think about paying it. The little girl enrolled in school, received a uniform like all the other children, started learning to read and write, and began eating lunch at the school every day.

Then there was the time I was with a team that was painting a house. I walked over to check on the team, and that's when I noticed her. She was hoeing in a garden. It looked like a rock garden because the ground was covered in rocks. But she was trying.

I soon learned that the lady had a husband who had recently become paralyzed from the waist down. He sits in a wheelchair all day long. She took me to meet him. He looked to be in his 50s, but it was hard to tell. Something terrible had happened. There was a pop, and he lost the use of his legs. He went to nine hospitals, but nothing had changed.

They have four children. Three are school age. The fourth, a daughter, died recently and left them with four grandchildren to care for. That gave them seven children to look after. All of this responsibility comes with no job (because there aren't any), no income (no disability check will come each month), and no hope (how will they survive).

I looked at them and didn't know what to do. I couldn't solve their problems. I couldn't make him walk. So I asked if I could pray for them. They're Christians and they said yes. So I prayed. I asked God for strength and healing and blessings. I said amen and lifted my eyes. Tears were rolling down his cheeks. He seemed to be a proud man, in a good way, and now he can't work his garden to provide food for his family.

An American named Janie texted me the following week. She had heard about this paralyzed man and his family. She wanted to know what they needed. I told her it would be great if two or three of the kids could be sponsored to go to the school there in the village. I told her it's $37 per month or $444 per year, for each child. They would get to eat every day and learn to read and write and do math. They would get a uniform and be like the other kids and have fun. And those would be two less meals for that mother to somehow provide each day.

Janie responded. I couldn't believe it. She asked if all seven needed to be sponsored. I said no. One is already in school, but six are not. She said to sign them all up. All six of them. She would send a check the next day. And she did.

They're in school now. All those children. I received word the mother was very excited when she got the news. She was thrilled to hear all these children would be in school each day. They would eat, get a uniform, and learn. They would have a chance.

And once again, one of God's children heard about the need. She had the means to help. And she did.

I love the story of Dieunal. He is a sweet little boy, about 5 years old, who lives in the remote village of Mathias. We began sponsoring children in his village to go to school in Thoman. He began to notice those children walking to school in their new uniforms, and he was unable to go because he had no sponsor. So, on his own, he walked over the mountain and knocked on the clinic door of our Hope Center. Laura, our missionary at the time, opened the door, and Dieunal asked her what he needed to do to be able to go to school. He didn't ask what she could do for him. He asked what he needed to do. His question broke Laura's heart, and she wasn't sure what to do. But God knew. Soon thereafter a dear lady from Colonial Heights Baptist Church in Ridgeland, MS became his sponsor. Now he goes to school every day with the other children from his village. He's getting an education and a meal every day. He's a serious little boy. He wants to be a doctor. And, he just might become one!

I WAS THINKING . . .

Don't forget this. When you get home, don't forget this.

That's what I told our group of twenty or so, mostly teenagers, this last Thursday as we sat in that tiny church high in the mountains of Haiti. There was no sound system, no video equipment. No fancy pews or theater seats. Just four walls made of sticks and dried mud, a few broken benches with no backs, and a table at the front.

As we sat there in silence, I became keenly aware that millions and millions of Jesus-followers all over the world sit in churches like that every week. They sing. They read scripture. They preach. They pray.

And sometimes they cry out. They cry out to God because they're hungry. Or they're sick. Or they're persecuted. They cry out to God for His grace and His mercy and His provision. They cry out for help.

So I told our little group not to forget. I told them to remember that church and remember those people. I told them to finish their education and get great jobs and support their families and then spend their time and their effort and their money making a difference in the lives of people who are hurting and suffering.

I told them there is more to life than acquiring things and then dying. I told them that in order to find their lives, they must lose them for the sake of the Gospel and the glory of Christ. I told them to die to self and then they'll live. Then they'll really, really live.

I think they will. At least some of them. They are a great group of kids from a Christian school in Sharpsburg, Georgia. They are smart and mature and committed to Christ.

I think they'll give and go and support. I think they'll make a difference. I really do.

If they don't forget.

CHAPTER 11

Starving Children

Rachel Charpie served in our orphanage for two years. Each day, the children of the orphanage would leave at 7:30 in the morning for school and not return until 2:30 in the afternoon. During that time, Rachel would wander up to the Hope Center and help in our medical clinic. Over time, she began to notice that many malnourished children were being brought to the clinic. She unintentionally developed an outpatient malnutrition program. She would measure the children, weigh them, and give them nutritious food called Plumpy Nut, which is a peanut butter based paste that is high in calories and nutrition. The children would return each week, and Rachel would weigh them, measure them, and give them more food. Before she knew it, Rachel had enrolled over 125 children in the outpatient program.

However, some children who came to the clinic needed more help then outpatient care. They needed inpatient care. Rachel would send them to an inpatient malnutrition center 2 1/2 hours away on the other side of Port-au-Prince. This was not good for the children or their families. Most of these families were desperately poor, lived in mud huts, and certainly had no means of transportation. They could not go see the children at the inpatient malnutrition center.

One week when I was in Haiti during the summer of 2016,

Rachel said to me, "We need our own inpatient malnutrition center."

I thought to myself, "No we don't." I knew this would be very costly and consume enormous amounts of time and resources. So, I said to her, "Send me an email. I want a detailed analysis of the cost of opening an inpatient facility as well as ongoing costs. In addition, I want to see the medical protocols we will use to admit patients, treat patients, evaluate their progress, and determine if they need to go to a full-scale hospital."

I was hoping this assignment would stymie Rachel. After all, the timing for this endeavor was terrible. I was about to send out a letter to our entire support base to raise $300,000 to build a new Hope Center in the Mississippi Delta. This was going to be our first big step in the States, and we needed to get it right. We did not need any distractions, especially in regard to fundraising. How on earth would we start a campaign to raise $300,000 with private funds and, at the same time, launch a different campaign to raise over $100,000 to begin an Inpatient Malnutrition Center? To make matters worse, about that time Hurricane Matthew roared through southwestern Haiti destroying towns and villages and wreaking havoc in a country that was already desperately poor. We needed to do something about the devastation from the hurricane because we were located east of the hurricane damage, had received no damage, and were in a position to help. But helping is not cheap. Helping often takes dollars, especially after a large natural disaster.

After a week or two, Rachel completed her proposal for an inpatient malnutrition center and prepared to send me the results of her research. Later, she would say that she had the email drafted, the attachments added, and wondered whether to hit the send button. Finally, she did, and shortly thereafter it landed in my inbox. Whereupon, I promptly ignored it. I pretended it was not there. I could tell from the subject line this was the email I had been dreading. I simply refused to open it. I was focused on the new Hope Center in the Mississippi Delta, and I did not want to be distracted. Nor did I want to divert funds from the Delta to another cause, no matter how worthy it might be.

Finally, I did open the email and discovered that it would cost at least $125,000 to begin the inpatient malnutrition center. That's exactly what I was afraid of. Now, what was I to do? Once again, I ignored the situation. I did not respond to Rachel. I gave her neither a yes nor a no. Later, Rachel would say that she prayed every day that God would not allow me to sleep or rest until I took action on this plan.

Why did Rachel pray this prayer? Why did she persist? Because she's a fighter. Rachel is tiny. She's barely 5 feet tall, if that. She has no financial resources of her own. But if I ever needed help, I'd want Rachel Charpie in my corner. As she was going through the process of trying to get the inpatient malnutrition center started, she wrote the following:

"If there was ever a doubt in my mind about why I am still in Haiti after 2 years, it was shattered this afternoon. Today a little boy died of malnutrition. He was 9 months old. The rest of the world will go on as normal, but his Mama won't forget. I refuse to forget. I refuse to let him be another statistic with no name or face. His name was Elison. And in his memory and for every child that comes after him, I will fight. No child should ever starve to death. It's an evil in this world that I will never understand. Elison's battle here on earth may have been lost, but his victory is in the arms of Jesus."

"I will fight." That's what she wrote. You see, there are some things worth fighting for. There are some things worth giving everything you've got. For Rachel, those "some things" are starving children in Haiti.

It was about that time I found myself on an airplane on a runway in Atlanta. I was traveling with my dad to Canton, Ohio. Earlier in the year he had turned 80 years old. For his birthday, I gave him a trip to the Pro Football Hall of Fame Induction

Ceremony in Canton, Ohio. That year, Brett Favre of Green Bay Packer fame was being inducted. Since I graduated from Southern Miss and saw Brett throw his first college pass back in 1987, and since my parents lived not far from the Southern Miss campus, we had followed Brett his entire career. I thought it would be a great weekend at the Hall of Fame and that turned out to be the case.

While on the runway in Atlanta waiting to take off, I was reading a book by Paul Farmer, a Harvard Doctor who has done great work in Haiti. His book was very inspiring, and I believe God used that book to stir me to action. Suddenly, I put down the book and picked up my phone. I sent a text to Rusty Hall, our BGM Managing Director, and told him the following: "We are going to open an inpatient malnutrition center. I have no idea how this is going to happen. But it is not a burden to raise money to feed starving children. That is a great privilege, and I can't wait to see how God is going to pull this off."

Three weeks later we had over $90,000 in the bank for the malnutrition center. But God! And by the way, during that time God and His people also sent over $300,000 for the new Hope Center in the Mississippi Delta as well as $100,000 for hurricane relief. But God, indeed!

In January of 2017, we began preparations to open our malnutrition center in Ganthier, Haiti, about 7 miles from our original Hope Center in Galette Chambon. We found a walled compound to rent, complete with a large house for the children and a separate house for Rachel and another missionary.

The malnutrition center is named Pen Lavi, which is Haitian Creole for "Bread of Life." I describe it as a mini-hospital. We have 15 full-time employees providing round-the-clock care. We have nurses and nannies and cooks. There is also a Haitian pediatrician who comes every other week to check on the children. If needed, we can take them to our medical clinic 7 miles away to be checked by our Haitian doctor or by our American nurse practitioner, Tony West.

We can take up to 12 children at a time and most of the children are from a few months old to 7 years old. The first year and a half of operation we had 80 children come through our program. One of the best parts of this ministry is that the mothers of the children are allowed to stay at the malnutrition center. Many of them are simply unaware of how to best care for their children. During their stay, they are given instructions and care and love. They are shown the best ways to care for their children and we have found this makes a profound difference in the lives of both the mothers and their children.

After the malnutrition center had been open for a few months, a young lady named Katie Ethridge moved to Haiti and joined Rachel full-time. Katie is from Birmingham, Alabama, graduated from nursing school at Ole Miss, and worked as an RN in Jackson, MS in the NICU unit at Blair E. Batson Children's Hospital. In the summer of 2016, Katie went on a mission trip to our Galette Chambon location with a group led by Dr. Mike McMullan and his wife, Missy. Mike, a cardiologist who teaches at the University of Mississippi School of Medicine, and Missy are wonderful Christian people who love to serve the Lord by serving others. Each year, they take a group of 26 medical students, nursing students, occupational therapy students, physical therapy students, doctors, and nurses on a mission trip with BGM to Haiti. Katie had been on the 2016 trip. Upon her return, she contacted me and said she felt God calling her to full-time medical missions work but she wasn't sure what that looked like. She believed her next step was to quit her job at the Children's Hospital and, starting in January of 2017, spend five months with BGM in Haiti. And that's what she did.

Katie spent the first couple of months at our Thoman location and the next three months at our Galette Chambon location. While in Galette Chambon, she began helping Rachel at the new malnutrition center. At the end of her 5 months in Haiti, she shared with us that she wanted to move to Haiti full-time and help Rachel run the malnutrition center. And that's what she did.

Working in a place like Haiti is not easy. People die from lack of nutrition, lack of shelter, or lack of medical care. Sometimes it would be easier not to love, especially when there is likely to be loss. Katie explained this in June of 2018 when she wrote the following about the mother of a malnourished child:

"Dear Carole, I owe you an apology. When you made your way into our lives two months ago, I didn't want to love you. I looked at your 75 lb. frame and counted your every bone. You were so fragile I was scared to sneeze for fear of blowing you away. I saw how easily your body tired and how lifeless your eyes stared back at mine. I held your tiny baby and prayed she would grow to know her mama. But I saw your lab results, I read the numbers, I knew your odds. They weren't good. You knew it too. We all did.

"I tried not to love you because I didn't want you to hurt me. It was easier to keep you at a distance. I now see how wrong that self-preservation mentality was, and I'm sorry. That's not Jesus. In fact, Jesus did the exact opposite on the cross . . . preserving none of Himself but draining every last drop instead. Do you remember how sick you were? My friend, you weren't the only one. The Lord has done miraculous things within us both since then. Our Healer made you stronger as He made me more vulnerable. He restored your body while He tore down my walls. He gave you energy and light and life where there was none. He gave us all hope. He gave us Himself.

"The breath in your lungs and the blood in your veins are not accidents. They are gifts. They are miracles that point us back to the Giver of all good gifts. So today as you walked out our doors with your healthy baby in your arms, we stood victorious for our Champion has made us whole. We stand in awe and give Jesus all the glory. Jesus, our Bread of Life."

Katie served with us for a year. She was an enormous help to Rachel. Not only did she provide expert medical care, but she was also a friend for Rachel. Her room was in the same building and down the hall from Rachel. They shared the joys and struggles of working together. It was a great situation for over a year. At the end of that year, in the fall of 2018, Katie announced that she was returning to the States to enter Nurse Practitioner school in Birmingham. At the same time, she became engaged to a young man who is doing mission work in Africa. Katie will be marrying him, completing school, and moving to Africa to help open and operate a medical clinic.

As He always does, God provided another Christian to take Katie's place at the Malnutrition Center. Her name is Jaimie. She was born 23 years ago in Haiti. Her mother died a few days after giving birth. Jaimie's father had other children and was desperately poor. He had no idea what to do with the new baby and no wife. A Canadian missionary couple living in Haiti at the time adopted Jaimie. They took her to Canada where she grew up, went to college, and became a nurse.

Around the age of 22, Jaimie became curious about her birth family. She discovered there was an American nurse who helped deliver her all those years ago in Haiti. The nurse was now living in Florida. Jaimie contacted her and, amazingly, the nurse not only remembered Jaimie's birth, but had a photo of Jaimie's mother holding Jaimie shortly after giving birth.

With information from the nurse, Jaimie was able to contact a private investigator In Haiti who helped locate her birth family. She has both full-siblings and half-siblings. Her father and mother had other children before Jaimie was born and then her father remarried and had other children. She has since become close with her siblings and their families.

In 2018, Jaimie moved to Haiti to work as a nurse at a malnutrition center near Port-au-Prince. She worked there for six or seven months and realized it was not a good fit for her. About that time, Katie had moved back to the States and we were looking for a nurse to take her place. Rachel interviewed Jaimie, Tony West interviewed her, then I interviewed her.

We believed her to be a strong Christian and a good fit for our organization. She came to work for us at our Malnutrition Center in the summer of 2019.

The children we serve through the Malnutrition Center are real people with real names and real families. There was Holanda. She weighed 4.4 lbs. when she was admitted but was soon weighing 13 lbs. Then there was Fanise. She arrived malnourished and swollen at 16.5 lbs. She lost her swelling and weighed 14.5 lbs. Then, she went home at a healthy 18.5 lbs.

In August of 2017, Rachel wrote, "Yesterday we welcomed Davernia, and today we welcomed Wendy into our care. We have gone from 3 to 8 children in a matter of a week. My prayer is not only for them to be healthy and grow, but also that they and their families will learn about Jesus and see His love in us. As I was speaking to Wendy's parents today, I explained to them that we are here because of Jesus – the dad told me he had already noticed the verses on the walls. I showed them the prayer wall and told them that people coming through to visit would be prayed for specifically. I am overwhelmed by all the responses of people praying for us! Thanks for fighting alongside us."

The children who are brought to the Malnutrition Center hear about us in a variety of ways. Some are already in our outpatient program at our two medical clinics. Their situations are not improving, so we send them to our Inpatient Center. Other clinics around Haiti also send patients to us. Some are like Kashme. He was 4 years old when he arrived and weighed only 17 lbs. A normal 4 year old should weigh between 40 and 45 lbs. After receiving healthy food and a lot of TLC, Kashme left as a happy little boy weighing 26 lbs. Then there was Charlie. In addition to being malnourished, he had cerebral palsy. This sweet little boy weighed only 16 lbs. at 5 years old. After many months, he gained weight and became healthy.

In February of 2018, I was on a trip to Haiti with one of our Board members, Rick Adams. We stopped by the Malnutrition

Center, and that's when we saw a heartbreaking situation. On a pillow in the playroom was a little boy. He was very small. I was shocked to learn that he was 6 years old. As he lay on his back, his knees were drawn and his hands were curled. I learned that he was both malnourished and afflicted with cerebral palsy. His mother has 9 children, all boys. Her husband had died a few months earlier. I cannot imagine her plight or the plight of her children. Her husband was dead, and she likely had very little education and few ways to earn an income. In addition, there are no social safety nets in Haiti. And, to make matters worse, she has a little boy with serious medical issues. She had taken him to different Malnutrition Centers, but they did not have the capacity to treat children with special needs. I was so happy to know that God had placed us there with the skills and abilities to help this precious child and his mother.

In April of 2018, I asked Rachel to give me an update on the work at Pen Lavi. She shared the following:

"Wow! God has done some crazy, awesome, amazing things over the last 10 months! Since opening in May of 2017, we have had 31 kids through our doors. Eight of those kids are currently with us. Except for a couple of slower times we have kept at least 8 kids with a steady flow of discharges and admits. We have had as many as 11 kids at one time.

"God has burdened our hearts not just for the kids we serve but for their families, too. We have some PRECIOUS mamas in our home right now. Somewhere along the way they become family and check on us as much as we care for them. Just last night we were out late with a patient at the hospital and our moms called to check and make sure we were okay. They heal as much as their children do, and we have many opportunities to share the gospel with them both in word and action. One mom came down from Thoman to stay with her son. See seemed indifferent to her child, and he didn't seem attached to her either. We just discharged them today, and there has been a dramatic change in their relationship. He cries if she's not there and there's a light in her eyes as she plays with him and loves him. The healing that took place in both of them while they were here was amazing!"

Sometimes the Malnutrition Center impacts people in ways we never imagined. Fenol was married and had 4 children. They lived in the mountains of Haiti until Fenol's wife became sick. Sadly, his wife died, and his two youngest children became very ill as a result of malnutrition. Then Fenol met Lovely, who has 2 children, one of whom was sick from malnutrition. Fenol and Lovely developed a relationship and had a child of their own. They were renting a horrible mud hut and living in deplorable conditions.

Fenol is a hard worker and desperately wanted a job. We hired him as the gardner/groundskeeper at the Malnutrition Center. He and Lovely wanted to get married but, as is common in Haiti, did not think they could get married because they could not afford to. We told them we could not provide a huge Haitian wedding and reception but we could help with a suit for Fenol and a dress for Lovely. They jumped at the chance and got married. In addition, they and their 6 children moved into a brand new house built by BGM. Everything changed for Fenol, Lovely, and their children. God brought them marriage, hope, a job, and a future. But God!

Millie Adams was a student at Mississippi State University. She had been to Haiti several times, including a one month stint as an intern. Millie saw the importance of malnourished children receiving Plumpy Nut. She saw how it was filled with calories and nutrition. So, Millie went back to school one semester and decided to raise funds so that we could provide more Plumpy Nut. As a college student with no job and no income other than what she received from her parents, Millie Adams raised $10,000 through a social media campaign. It was incredible!

Two years later, Millie graduated from Mississippi State and was living in Memphis. She emailed me one day and told me that she learned from Rachel Charpie that we spend about

$700 every month on Plumpy Nut. That is, of course, $8,400 per year. She said it was her goal to raise a year's worth of Plumpy Nut. Millie created an incredible social media campaign, complete with humor and stories, and within a matter of weeks had raised over $8,600, enough to supply all of our Plumpy Nut for a year. I simply love it when young people take the initiative and figure out how to make a difference!

Over the years we have shied away from doing fundraisers for BGM. We do not do carwashes or pancake sales. We have found that often times those types of events take an enormous amount of time and energy for very little return. In 2019 we have a budget of $2.6 million. It would be very difficult to have the typical fundraising events to provide that kind of funding.

However, we decided to have a fundraising event in May 2019 for our Malnutrition Center. The Malnutrition Center is one of two ministries we have that are non-revenue producing. The other one is our Montessori school in the Delta. Starving two-year olds who live in mud huts don't bring a lot of money when they are admitted to the malnutrition center. Therefore, all the of the funds to operate the center must be raised. The annual budget in 2019 for the malnutrition center was $127,000.

Dina Ray, our development director, suggested that we have an event to raise part of the budget. At first, I was reluctant because of the reasons listed above. However, she made a strong case, and we decided to move forward. The plan was to have a sponsored event that included an online auction and a dinner. Broadmoor Baptist Church graciously agreed to allow us to have the event at their church. We sold over 300 tickets for the event, brought in Pastor Mathurin from Haiti to talk about issues of poverty and hunger, as well as Rachel Charpie to talk about the Malnutrition Center.

Our initial goal was $85,000. Our "hallelujah" goal was the entire $127,000 budget. When all was said and done, we raised over $173,000 with only $10,000 in expenses. But God!

I WAS THINKING . . .

It was a tough year. Really tough. His wife of over 40 years passed away. He retired from the collegiate ministry they had done together for decades. Then he moved to a new state to be near his daughter and her family. Any one of those would have been enough, but all three at the same time was almost too much to bear.

When she died about seven months ago, the family had an idea. She had been to Haiti on mission trips many times. So, instead of flowers, they asked people to donate funds in her name to build a house in a remote village.

And they did. Lots of people. Lots of people who had been blessed by her life and ministry for decades gave enough money to build a house. The house was built for an older lady living in squalid conditions in a mud hut with no resources and no hope.

This past Wednesday he and his daughter and his son-in-law and one of his sons and two of his granddaughters hiked to that house. They painted it a bright green Caribbean-like color. And it was beautiful. The sweet Haitian lady was so happy. She thanked them over and over. Of course, tears were shed. Lots of tears. Then they hung a plaque inside the house in his wife's memory. And they thought about their wife/mother/grandmother and how pleased she would be.

Then Thursday night the little Haitian lady walked down the mountain and came to church. The family who painted her house walked up to the platform and sang "Victory in Jesus" and "Power in the Blood." And there were more tears. And a tough year became a little better.

CHAPTER 12

Mississippi Delta

When we began our work in Haiti, it was always in the back of my mind that we would go to Haiti, learn some principles of community development and come back to our home state of Mississippi and apply these principles. After all, we have a few problems of our own.

But where in Mississippi would we work? We knew we wanted to be in Mississippi and we knew we wanted to be in the Delta, but the Delta covers a large part of the map. In fact, the Mississippi Delta runs from Memphis down to Vicksburg, and from I-55 to the Mississippi River. There are large numbers of counties and towns throughout the Delta that could use a helping hand. How would we decide which one?

Our Managing Director at BGM, Rusty Hall, and I decided to drive through the Delta, pray as we go, and look for signs of health. Those signs would include a medical clinic, a dental clinic, a hospital, a bank, a grocery store, good schools, active churches, competent government agencies, and other factors. If we saw signs of health in a town, we would know that town was not for us. We needed to go where the need was the greatest.

So, we got out a map and planned our trip through the Delta. On the day of the big trip, we drove to Hernando, Mississippi to meet with Tom Pittman and get his counsel. Tom is the long-time Director of the Community Foundation of Northwest Mississippi. While having lunch, Tom said we should go to Jonestown, Mississippi and meet with Sister Teresa. I've been in Mississippi for 52 years. I had never heard of Jonestown. I thought Jonestown was where Jim Jones and his followers drank the Kool-Aid and committed suicide in South America all those years ago! Tom assured us there is a Jonestown, Mississippi. As it turns out Jonestown has a population of approximately 1,500, all of whom are African-American. And Sister Teresa was a Catholic nun who had been working there for over 30 years.

Rusty and I left Tom and located Jonestown on the map. We drove into town and came to a series of dilapidated storefronts that were the heart of downtown Jonestown. It was mid-afternoon by that time, and I wanted some chocolate. At first, I wasn't sure if the store where we parked was open, but it was. I entered the store and the floor beneath me creaked. I purchased a candy bar and a soft drink and learned that Sister Teresa was down the street at the Jonestown Family Center (JFC).

Rusty and I walked into JFC and were greeted warmly by Sister Teresa Shields. She was the Director of JFC and had given leadership there for 30 years. JFC consisted of a Toddler Program for 2 year olds, a Montessori for 3-5 year olds, and a fitness center.

Sister Teresa shared with us the history of the program as well as some of the challenges. She then asked what we do and what we were planning to do in the Delta. We told her about our work in Haiti and how we planned to bring those concepts to the Delta, including hosting teams. Sister Teresa said, "So you'll bring a team or two to the Delta during the summer?"

I responded, "Sister Teresa, I have to be perfectly honest. We'll bring teams every week of the summer and many other weeks throughout the year." She was shocked. Mississippi is a predominantly Protestant state. Therefore, there were not many

Mississippi churches going to Jonestown to partner with Sister Teresa and the other nuns who were primarily from the Pacific Northwest. Each year, they had a few teams from Wisconsin, New York, and other places outside of Mississippi. On the other hand, BGM consists of people who grew up in Mississippi, live in Mississippi, and go to church in Mississippi. We know many churches throughout the state. And, as we always say, Mississippi is a club, not a state. Everyone knows everyone. Thus, we would be able to bring a large number of mission teams to Jonestown.

We continued our visit at JFC, and then Rusty and I left to continue our tour of the Delta. We went through many Delta towns, talked with mayors as well as local citizens, and then concluded our trip.

Over the next few days and weeks, Jonestown kept coming to our minds. There had not been many signs of health - no medical clinic, no dental clinic, no pharmacy, no bank, no grocery store, and very few jobs. It was our kind of place!

Eventually, we met the mayor, Patrick Campbell. We hit it off immediately with Patrick. He was a graduate of Jackson State, a smart guy, and was aware of the needs in the community. Patrick told us he believed we should come to Jonestown. I told him, "That's what you believe. But what about the rest of the community?"

He said, "I'll call a meeting of community leaders, and you can share your vision. Then we'll see what they think."

When we met Patrick, we also met Ms. Pearline. She had been the town clerk for 42 years. Ms. Pearline knew everybody and everything about Jonestown. She had seen it all. Ms. Pearline was very welcoming and was an incredible source of information, especially as we were getting started. She told us how things worked, who we should talk to, and how to contact them.

A few weeks after meeting with Patrick and Ms. Pearline, we drove to Jonestown for the meeting. Rusty Hall and Buddy

Huff, our Board President, went with me. Two professors from the Ole Miss McLean Institute, Albert Nylander and J. R. Love, came to the meeting. We had been consulting with them for months about our proposed work in the Delta, and they were a huge help. We arrived at the community center where I set up my computer and projector, and the room began to fill. Law enforcement officers, government officials, educators, business people, and members of the clergy attended the meeting.

I shared a PowerPoint presentation and told about BGM, our work in Haiti, and proposals for working in Jonestown. At the end of the presentation, I asked if there were any questions. A lady on the front row raised her hand. I called on her and she asked, "What do we have to do to pass the test for y'all to come?"

I said, "What did you say?"

She repeated the question. "What do we have to do to pass the test for y'all to come."

I said, "There's no test. If y'all think it's a good idea and we think it's a good idea, then we'll pray about it and see if it's a good fit."

There were a few other questions, and then we adjourned. Buddy Huff was standing at the door as people exited the room. One local pastor said to Buddy, "I was glad to hear that man talk about partnering with people here in Jonestown. We've had people come into our community and tell us what we were going to do. And they never even bothered to ask us what we wanted to do."

Several days later I went to that pastor's home. I thanked him for coming to the meeting and asked him about his background and his years of service at his church. Then I told him I had heard what he said about us partnering together. I said, "Pastor, I cannot imagine telling someone what they are going to do instead of finding ways to partner with them." I continued, "We know we have to earn your trust and the trust of the people of Jonestown. We also know that will take time, but we intend to earn that trust and we intend to be here for the long haul." Sometime later that Pastor invited me to preach at his church, and we had a great time worshiping together.

In addition to searching for a community that had fewer signs of health, we had three other criteria we used when determining where to go. First, we wanted to go where God was working. In John 5, Jesus said He was simply working where the Father was already working. That's what we wanted to do. We wanted to join God in what He was already doing. As we examined Jonestown, we could see that God was already working there, and we wanted to be part of what He was doing.

Second, we wanted to go where there was a man or woman of peace. In Luke 10, Jesus sent 72 followers, two by two, into the towns where He would be going. He told them to enter a town and find a man of peace. This was a very practical instruction because it would be enormously helpful for His followers to find a person who shared their beliefs and values. We found numerous people in Jonestown who wanted to move forward and who shared our beliefs.

Third, we wanted to go to where the town wanted to partner with us. In Matthew 10:14, Jesus sent forth His 12 disciples and told them if they entered a town and the people did not welcome them, then they should shake the dust off their feet and go to a different town. We had no desire to fuss with people. We do not want to be in constant conflict with people. We want to be in a town where the people want to partner with us for the betterment of the community. As demonstrated in the meeting we held with the community leaders, we found a town that was eager to partner with us.

BGM APPROACH

Once we nailed down the location in the Delta where we would work, we had to ask an important question. How would our work make a difference? Billions of dollars have been spent over the years in the Delta with limited results. Why would our work be any different?

We believe our approach is different for several reasons. First, we are **Christ-centered**. We believe that a relationship with God that comes through faith in Jesus Christ not only gets us to heaven, but it also teaches us how to live here on Earth. God's word is very practical. The Old Testament book of Proverbs addresses many of the issues we face today. It warns us about ungodly friends, sexual misconduct, alcohol consumption, and laziness, to name a few. I have found that whenever I am in a bind, I realize that if I had done things God's way, I would probably not be in that terrible situation. In fact, we could go to any prison in America and the inmates would have to admit that if they had done life God's way they probably wouldn't be in that prison. Further, we are convinced that changing hearts and minds is vital to long-term change and success. We can provide medical care, quality schools, decent housing, and even jobs. But if people have serious character flaws, if they don't exhibit the fruit of the Spirit such as love, joy, peace, patience, kindness, goodness, faithfulness, gentleness, and self-control, then nothing we do will last. The community will not experience lasting change.

Second, we have a **holistic approach** to our work. We don't work in only one area or two areas. Our SPHERES approach allows us to work in the 7 areas we believe are necessary to have a healthy community. We believe this is extremely important. After all, it would be nice if a person gets access to medical care, but what if she goes home to a house that is falling apart, and she can see through the floor all the way to the ground? That would be terrible. We believe all people need spiritual care, medical care, clean water, a good education, decent housing, jobs, and access to healthy food.

Third, we are a **Mississippi-based** organization. We're not going anywhere. We're not leaving. We're already home.

Groups from other states have gone to Jonestown in the past. They have stayed for a week and done good work. But they had to go home. They have jobs and families and responsibilities back home. They can only come once a year because they live hundreds and hundreds of miles away. On the other hand, we can drive to Jonestown any day of the week and many times throughout the month. We're close. We're nearby. And we're not going anywhere. Moreover, I told our board it would be criminal if we didn't do something about the troubles in our own state. This is our state, and we should be doing something about the problems that are here. Further, I believe God must be saying to us, "What more can I give you people? I've given you resources, education, contacts, skills, abilities, and everything necessary to make a significant difference right where you live. Do something!"

Fourth, we believe in having **boots-on-the-ground**. If you are going to make a significant, long-term impact, you have to be there. It's very difficult to bring positive, lasting change from afar. It's hard to influence people in a personal way if you are not there with them. Change takes time. Relationships take time. Trust takes time. Moreover, from a practical and organizational standpoint, someone who understands our work must be present to implement the programs and ministries we offer.

Fifth, we believe in having a **permanent presence**. Not only does someone from the organization need to be here, but that person needs to be there permanently. We can't have someone popping in once a month or every few months. That will not work. We need someone who moves into the community and lives full-time among the people.

Sixth, we believe in the impact of **weekly teams**. Mission teams can be distracting and even harmful to a community if they are not handled properly. However, when they function properly, they can have a very big and very positive impact in a community. Teams bring energy, enthusiasm, human resources, financial resources, and ideas. Exposure to the needs of the community will enable people to become more involved. I've been in Mississippi over 50 years, but I had never heard of Jonestown until the day we met with Tom Pittman. I had never helped in Jonestown because I did not know Jonestown existed. The same is true for many other people in Mississippi and beyond. They can't help if they are unaware of the needs. They can't provide direction and resources if they've never seen or heard of the community. Countless times in Haiti we have had someone show up on a mission trip. They look around and say, "Have you ever thought about doing such and such?"

We say, "No, we haven't. But we'd like to."

And they say, "That's what my company does. We'd love to implement this and pay the costs to make it happen." We've seen that scene play out countless times.

Seventh, we believe in the **collaboration** of the church, universities, and private businesses. This is the winning formula. Rarely, if ever, does it fail. The church has the largest base of volunteers in the world. There are 2 billion of us. Universities bring students who are enthusiastic and not yet jaded about the world. They bring the latest technology, professors, research, and influential alumni. Private business owners get the job done. If they don't, they go out of business. We've seen this combination numerous times, and it always works.

BUILDING THE DELTA TEAM

Kelly Sayle was a Middle School Minister at Silverdale Baptist Church in Chattanooga, TN in 2015. She had been there five years and believed God was leading her in a new direction. She wanted to do some type of holistic ministry in the Mississippi Delta, but she didn't know what that looked like. Kelly had grown up in the Delta in Greenville, MS. She graduated from Delta State University and then went to Southwestern Baptist Theological Seminary in Ft. Worth, TX. After graduating from Southwestern, she returned to work at her home church in Greenville for a few years, then went to a church plant outside Atlanta before landing in Chattanooga.

A friend of Kelly knew Kelly was trying to find God's direction for her life, so she told Kelly about a conference in Nashville. Thousands of mostly young people attended the conference to talk about future missions possibilities. Kelly showed up, and they immediately asked if she was interested in international work or North American work. Kelly told them North American, and she was shown to a room to talk with someone. A man named George Ross was there talking with people about work in North America. Kelly explained that she thought she might be interested in the Mississippi Delta, but she wasn't sure. George lived in New Orleans and trained church planters. He also hosted mission teams in the city. He invited Kelly to come to New Orleans and see what they were doing since she didn't know exactly what she wanted to do. George was hosting church staff members from around the country on a tour of mission possibilities. Kelly agreed to go.

A few weeks later Kelly was on a tour bus in New Orleans with pastors and church staff members from around the country. Sitting directly across from her was a man named Rob Futral. Rob was the Senior Pastor at Broadmoor Baptist Church in Madison, MS. I'm a member of Broadmoor and Rob was my pastor. Kelly and Rob began talking, and Rob asked her, "Why are you here on this tour?"

Kelly responded, "I'm not sure. I really want to work in the Mississippi Delta, but I don't know what that looks like."

Rob said, "Do you know my friend, Stan Buckley?" Kelly said she had heard the name but thought I was doing international work. Rob told her that I had been doing work in Haiti, but I was beginning a new work in the Mississippi Delta. Kelly wasn't sure what to do next. Should she ask Rob for my contact information? She noticed Rob had begun typing on his phone. She finally asked if he had my contact information. Rob said, "Sure. I'm texting with him right now."

A week later I was on a phone call with Kelly. I was sitting in my car in a parking lot in front of a Subway restaurant. We talked for an hour as she shared what God had placed on her heart and the desire she had to return to the Delta. She then asked about our work. I told her the story of BGM and our work in Haiti. I shared how we have two Hope Centers there and how we do all of our work through those Hope Centers. Kelly said, "That's very interesting. I have a piece of paper where I've been writing down aspects of ministry in which I might be interested. One of the items is Hope Center."

Kelly seemed like a good fit for BGM and our work in the Delta. She shared that she was going to Greenville, MS to visit with her parents in a couple of weeks. We arranged for Buddy Huff, our Board President, and me to meet Kelly along I-55 near Grenada, MS at a hotel restaurant. We met, and all three of us sensed this might be a good fit.

A few weeks later, I invited Kelly to our office in Ridgeland to continue our discussions. This was a very important position, and we had to get it right. Kelly came to our office, met some of our staff, and then we went to a local restaurant to meet with several Board members. As we sat down at the restaurant, I introduced Kelly to some of our Board members, including Mark Rich. I noticed she was looking strangely at Mark. Finally, after we had talked for a while, Kelly looked and Mark and said, "Where are you from?"

He said, "Greenville."

She said, "What school did you go to?" He told her. Then she said, "I thought you looked familiar. I went to that same school until 10th grade, and then I transferred." Then they talked about Greenville and all the people with whom they had gone to school. I wasn't surprised. Remember, Mississippi is a club, not a state!

Kelly joined our team full-time in September of 2016. There are very limited housing options in Jonestown, so she moved to Clarksdale which is only 10 miles from Jonestown. It's a very easy commute each day to work and minister in Jonestown.

We started hosting teams in Jonestown in 2017. We had not yet built our Hope Center, so teams stayed in an old Habitat for Humanity team house in Clarksdale. Eleven teams came to Jonestown during 2017, stayed in Clarksdale, and drove to Jonestown each day to work.

We knew our new Hope Center would open in January of 2018, and we knew we would have many more teams coming to Jonestown to serve. We also knew we needed a Team Host to help with all the teams that were signing up. A couple named Dennis and Veronica Hicks were introduced to us through mutual friends. We needed someone who was good with details. Dennis had recently retired from the Miss. Air National Guard after working 28 years in logistics and maintenance. We interviewed Dennis and Veronica and they became part of the BGM team the first of 2018 and moved to the Delta just a few miles from Jonestown.

Our team was coming together, but we needed one more person. Enter Linda McGrew. Linda was a native of Jonestown. She had been in that area her entire life. For many years Linda had hosted an after-school program for elementary children. When Kelly moved to Jonestown, Linda befriended her and became a person on whom Kelly could rely. About the time we were hiring Dennis and Veronica, we began interviewing Linda as our Life Center Coordinator. Her job, in part, was to open our new Life Center each day and provide information for the residents of Jonestown. At the Life Center, a former bank building, she shares our ministries with people in Jonestown. For example, we have a legal clinic there and a high school diploma program. People who are interested in applying for a loan for a new house will go to the Life Center to start the process. Also, our dental clinic is open every Friday. So, if a person on Tuesday wants to make an appointment for Friday, he would go to the Life Center on Tuesday and make that appointment since he could not go to the dental clinic on Tuesday to make the appointment.

HOPE CENTER

Randy Cress and his wife, Faye, are long-time members of Colonial Heights Baptist Church in Ridgeland, Mississippi. I was serving as the Interim Pastor of Colonial Heights in 2015 when Randy said to me, "I've recently retired. I need a project." Boy, did I have a project!

Randy grew up in Hattiesburg, Mississippi, graduated from Auburn University as a veterinarian, and moved to Tennessee to set up a practice. After 15 or 20 years working as a veterinarian, Randy moved back to Mississippi and built custom houses for the next 25 years in the Madison County area.

When Randy informed me that he needed a project, I immediately thought of our plans for the new Hope Center in Jonestown. We had to have a general contractor, someone who could guide us all the way from the planning process to the finished building. Little did I know that Randy Cress would be the perfect person to guide us through the building process.

Not only did we need a general contractor before we could start building the Hope Center, we also needed the funds to pay for it. We didn't have one penny for the Hope Center when we committed to working in Jonestown. However, in September of 2016, we raised $105,000 towards a goal of $240,000 to build the Hope Center. That $105,000 came from three individual donors and Broadmoor Baptist Church.

Then, on October 10, we sent a letter to our donor base asking them to help us raise the remaining $135,000. As they always do, our BGM supporters came through. Individual donors gave over $100,000. Then, Pinelake Church of Flowood, MS (with campuses in Clinton, Madison, Starkville, and Oxford) made us one of the recipients of their annual Christmas offering. In January of 2017, Pinelake sent us a check for $102,000. God had provided over $300,000 in cash in a matter of months to build the new Hope Center. And that was important because that's how much we ended up spending on construction. But God!

Not only did we need funds to build the new Hope Center, but we also needed land on which to build it. I thought that would be the easy part. I was wrong! BGM and I like to move quickly. We don't deal well with red tape. We are anti-bureaucracy. So, when month after month passed and we still didn't have land, I was very frustrated. The challenge was that much of the land in which we were interested had liens on it. We certainly were not going to spend money on a new building on land that didn't have good title.

That's when God stepped in again, this time in the form of Bubba Weir. Bubba is one of God's people. Like Randy, he was a member of Colonial Heights Baptist Church. Bubba had spent years working for a government agency that helped bring new businesses to small towns. He knew lots of people in lots of places. Bubba told us about a lawyer/businessman in Clarksdale, Mississippi that might be of help. The man's name was John Cocke. We met with John at a restaurant in Clarksdale. We told John what we were already doing in Jonestown and how we had raised the funds to build the Hope Center, but we couldn't find any land on which to build it. John said, "How much land do you need?"

I said, "About 150 ft. by 150 ft."

John said, "We can do that." As it turns out, John's family was originally from Jonestown. They had owned land there for generations. John had good title.

I replied to John, "How much will that cost us?"

John said, "Not a thing. You can have it." And that's how we got the land where the Hope Center sits today. But God!

When I first approached Randy, we only had a general idea

of what the building would look like. In fact, when Randy came to our office to talk about it, I drew the building on a piece of paper with a pencil. What we knew at the time was that we needed dorm space for our teams, a larger gathering area, a big kitchen, a conference room, and office space for our Community Manager. But we needed plans, real plans. Randy especially needed construction drawings. So, he called Tim Taylor, an architect with whom he had worked previously. Tim prepared fantastic drawings and didn't charge a dime. But God!

As we continued making plans, Randy, a strong and mature Christian, was beginning to see God work in ways that he not seen Him work previously. Randy kept asking where we would get subcontractors to go to the Mississippi Delta and how much did we want to pay them. I assured Randy that we had lots of Christian friends who would help. I also assured him that God had people we didn't even yet know about. Then I told Randy about another saying we have at BGM: God has people. God has all kinds of people. He has nurses, plumbers, accountants, electricians, doctors, dentists, carpenters, farmers, business owners, pastors, and any other category you can name. God has people! And they're great, and awesome, and giving. God has people!

Already, God had provided people in the form of Bubba Weir and Tim Taylor and John Cocke. I was convinced that God would provide others as we launched out in obedience to build the new Hope Center.

We were going to have a significant amount of plumbing work done. Of course, for BGM there was only one call to make – to Mike and Jann Kenney, owners of Quality Plumbing in Jackson, Mississippi and the ones who have done all of our plumbing work in Haiti. They are simply the best! Mike and Jann spent weeks in Jonestown planning and installing a large amount of pipes and fixtures. The Hope Center has 11 toilets, 11 showers, two continuous hot water systems, 12 sinks, and a large automatic ice maker. Patton Ford accompanied Mike and

Jann when they started the project, and his brother, Crocket Ford, helped at the end. As always, Mike and Jann asked for nothing for their efforts. God has people!

We needed lots of concrete for the slab. Our friend, Shane Huff, works for a company that sells concrete. Of course, he couldn't give us the concrete, nor did we ask him to, but he worked with his company to give us the best deal possible, and then they delivered it perfectly and in a timely manner. God has people!

We knew we needed framers for this 6,000 sq. ft. facility. I called a construction owner in McComb who had helped us several years earlier in Haiti and asked if he had framers. He said he had gotten away from having his own framing crews and just hired them wherever he was building. But, he suggested that I call Jerry McBride in Southaven, MS and tell Jerry that he had told us to call. I started to call Jerry and then I said to Randy, "Why don't you call him? I don't even know the building terms to use when I talk to him." Randy agreed to call him.

Randy reached Jerry, told him what we were doing, and Jerry said, "It's funny you are calling today. We just had a meeting here at the office and we were discussing how God has really blessed our business lately and we should do something to give back." And he did. He sent a framing crew that stayed for two weeks and completed all of the framing. He was going to charge us for nothing but the materials.

One day while their crews were doing the framing, I called one of Jerry's sons who works at the company. I thanked him for what they were doing and expressed how it was a huge help to us. He responded, "We believe your organization is really good at sharing the gospel and providing medical care and an education and jobs. We're really good at building things. So, we figured if we do what we're good at then that might help you do what you're good at."

I said, "That sounds exactly like what the Apostle Paul was talking about when he said there are different parts of the body but each one is important. We all have different roles but all the roles count in God's eyes." Shortly thereafter, Jerry told us he was sending us a bill for $14,000 for some of the materials. He told us to pay the bill, and then he was going to make a $14,000 donation to BGM. God has people!

We needed some more 2 x 4's for the Hope Center. Tommy Stansell with Southeast Timber Products donated a large amount of lumber. Tommy is in business with his father-in-law, Billy Van Devender, and his brother-in-law, William Van Devender, who have been instrumental in our work. God has people!

As you can imagine, there was an enormous amount of electrical work that needed to be done. Once again, God had just the right person. Milton Palmer owns a successful electrical company in Petal, MS. He and his wife, Becky, have supported BGM for many years. Milton personally came to Jonestown on two different occasions, brought his best crew, and charged us nothing for all that labor. We paid only for materials. God has people!

Then there was Eric Winter, another member of Colonial Heights. One Sunday after church, Eric walked up to me and asked how many windows we had at the new Hope Center. I had no idea what he did for a living, so I thought it was a strange question. I told him I wasn't sure but I could find out. Then I asked him why he had asked that question. He said, "I have a company that makes and sells blinds. We want to make and install the blinds at no cost." God has people!

We can't forget Ron Windom, yet another member of Colonial Heights. Ron and his crews donated and installed three large flat screen televisions, including one in our conference room and one in the great room. They ran all the wire for those screens as well as for our internet service. He never charged a penny. God has people!

While we are still discussing Colonial Heights, there are others. Howard Hornsby and Kevin Williams of the Burns Cooley

Dennis engineering firm conducted all of the soil samples and testing at no cost. Greg Brown, another engineer, spent a day with Randy wrecking forms and doing other work. Drew Baum and his father-in-law, Allen, purchased all of the cabinets at cost and charged nothing for the installation. Ron Willet and two lifegroups helped paint the outside of the Hope Center. Will Edgar brought a crew and did the outside landscaping. God has people!

There was Thomas Rico of Oxford, MS. Thomas painted the entire inside of that large building and charged only one-half the cost of his labor. God has people!

Finally, we had the building completed, but we had no furniture. I contacted my friend Tommy Miskelly of Miskelly Furniture. They have a huge furniture business in central Mississippi that draws customers from all over the South. Tommy talked to his brothers, Oscar and Chip, and they agreed that our Hope Center would be one of their big charitable projects for the year. We ordered 20 bunk beds, 20 mattresses, two couches, two chairs, and a double bed frame and mattress. When the mattresses arrived, they were the best mattresses Miskelly sells. They are extremely comfortable! When it was totaled, the furnishings had a normal retail value of $55,000. We paid only $5,000. God has people!

All of these amazing people enabled us to have a building that should have cost $600,000 but only cost $300,000. Randy complied the numbers so that we could see what an incredible blessing God's people were during the construction of the Hope Center.

As can be seen, many people sacrificed to make the Hope Center possible. But it would not have been possible without the overall vision and leadership of Randy Cress. It's no exaggeration to say that Randy gave a year of his life to build the Hope Center. His attention to detail and his refusal to cut corners or do anything with less than excellence made all the difference.

One more thing about the Hope Center. It's not just a building. It's far more than that. It's a tool to be used for God's glory and the benefit of others. It is out of the Hope Center that all of our work emanates. Mission teams are investing in the community; Bible studies are being held; children are being educated; dental patients are being treated; houses are being planned; jobs are being created; and lives are being touched.

JOBS

When you do this kind of work long enough, you begin to realize that without the creation of jobs, the only thing left is a hand-out. At BGM, we are not a give-away organization. We don't think constant give-aways are good for the giver or the recipient. Moreover, it's not sustainable.

Jobs, then, are the key. Jobs give dignity. Jobs enable people to support themselves and their families. Jobs provide food, clothing, housing, and the basics of life. I have seen this play out in my own life. I have had a very good life in terms of housing, transportation, education for myself and my children, travel, and many more things. Aside from the grace of God, the reason I have had these things is because I've had a full-time job my entire adult life. So, we know jobs are an essential part of a happy and productive life. That's why economic development is very important to our work.

One day I was visiting with Jerry Gibson, the owner of Capital Bolt and Screw which is located in Ridgeland, Mississippi. Jerry has been very supportive of our work in Haiti over the years. While we were talking about our new work in the Delta, I told Jerry that we can build houses and educate children and treat patients, but the most difficult thing we do is build an economy out of nothing. The hardest thing to do is to create jobs. Jerry said, "I have some jobs I can send up there right now."

After I picked myself up off the concrete, I asked Jerry what he was talking about. He explained that he has certain clients who want nuts and bolts placed in little bags. For example, if you buy an item that comes in a box, and the item must be put together, you will find inside the box a small bag of screws. Those screws don't get into the bag by themselves. Some of Jerry's clients who purchase screws from him want to outsource the process of putting the screws in the bags.

Several months after my conversation with Jerry, we hired four people in Jonestown for temporary jobs putting screws in bags. Four people worked two days, and each person made $250. That's pretty good money in the Delta for unskilled labor!

In early 2019, Jerry's son, Brian, called me to say they had secured a large job involving hundreds of thousands of bags that would take many months to complete. We could start by hiring two people: a supervisor and a worker. Each worker is paid by the "piece." In other words, they are paid per bag. The faster they work, the more money they make per hour. The pace is up to each worker.

One of the workers is a single mom in her later 30's. Her name is Cassie. The other worker is her younger brother, Cordaryl. Cassie is the Supervisor and can earn the equivalent of $11.50 to $15 per hour, depending on how many bags she fills. Cordaryl can earn the equivalent of $10.50 to $14 per hour, depending on how many bags he fills.

Our goal is that by the beginning of 2020, we will help Cassie form her own company and hire workers to place the screws in the bags. We project that Cassie could start off making $36,000 per year and then grow her business from there. We believe there are other companies who need similar work done, and we want to have that work done in Jonestown, Mississippi.

Another goal we have is to build an economic development center. This building will be a 3,000 square-foot warehouse that can be expanded in the future. I have a friend who owns a construction company, and he has offered to build the warehouse at cost. This economic center is crucial to future job growth. Right now, if we sit down with potential employers to provide jobs in Jonestown, we have nowhere for them to come. We want to be able to tell them that we have a place they can come at no cost, or little cost, complete with a loading dock and a forklift.

One of our goals has been to leverage our connections and reputation to help land jobs in Jonestown. I've often thought that if the mayor of Jonestown was by himself sitting across the table from a business owner that he was trying to lure to Jonestown, the mayor would be in a difficult position. However, it might be helpful if I was sitting beside the mayor and so were some of our board members as well as the president of the nearby community college. And perhaps we would even know the business owner. We could say to him, "Come to Jonestown. Bring jobs to this area. This is our state. This is your state. Let's do something about the challenges that are here. We are here in Jonestown. We know the people. We know the workers. They will do a good job. They will show up on time. They will be sober. They will not cheat you. You will be pleased. Bring jobs to Jonestown!" It seems we may be in a better position to attract businesses if we do it together rather than if the mayor has to do it alone.

As of this writing, we are providing ten jobs in Jonestown. Seven are at our school, one works at our Life Center, and two are doing the work for Capital Bolt & Screw. This is only a start, but it is a start. As these workers prove how good they are, we firmly believe we will be able to attract other businesses to Jonestown.

DENTAL CARE

Many years ago the Henry-Schein company had a mobile dental unit they took around the country to showcase the latest dental equipment. It was a very sophisticated $1.5 million mobile unit. Following hurricane Katrina, they put the mobile unit on the Mississippi Gulf Coast to allow local dentists to get their practices up and running. After a number of years, the unit was no longer needed on the Coast and the company donated it to the Mississippi Department of Health. For some reason, the Department of Health placed the unit in Jonestown. It was used for a period of time until parts of the unit broke and they stopped using it.

When we arrived in Jonestown, we thought it would be a good idea to get the broken pieces fixed and reopen the unit. As it turned out, getting the dental clinic open was more complicated than we imagined. We had to make certain repairs on the unit. We had to purchase an electronic medical records system. We spent approximately $20,000 getting the clinic ready to open.

These challenges were much different than what we faced in Haiti. In Haiti in the rural areas, you can simply pull up a chair and allow dentists to start pulling teeth. It doesn't work that way in America! There are countless rules and regulations of the health department that must be followed. The health department was very cooperative and gave a long-term lease of the unit for $1 per year. We then jumped through all the hoops and were finally able to get the clinic open.

Currently, the clinic is open every Friday with volunteer dentists. We have some wonderful dentists from across the state who have volunteered to give of their time. They will normally bring a hygienist or dental assistant with them. The state has graciously provided an assistant who works every Friday with our volunteer dentists. We have all the dental equipment on-site so that the dentists need to bring only themselves.

In addition, Linda McGrew from our Life Center schedules all the dentists as well as the patients. Of all the things we have done in Jonestown, the people seem to be most excited about the dental clinic. I suppose that makes sense because there are few things worse than a toothache! We currently have 110 people on a waiting list to see a dentist. There is no charge to come to the dental clinic. Initially, we thought we would charge at least a small amount based on a sliding scale. However, the unit is owned by the Health Department and their regulations forbid us from charging anything.

Importantly, in January of 2019, we entered into a formal agreement with the University of Mississippi School of Dentistry. This agreement allows their students and faculty to serve at our clinic.

MEDICAL CARE

There was a medical clinic in Jonestown until 2005 when the last provider left. The town owns the building where the clinic was located. After the clinic closed, the building was used for an after-school program for elementary children. Shortly after we arrived in Jonestown, the after-school program closed, and we acquired a long-term lease for the building.

The clinic was built in 1962 and after years of neglect desperately needed updating. Randy Cress, the man who built our Hope Center, and a crew of skilled volunteers from Ridgecrest Baptist Church in Madison, Mississippi began renovating the medical clinic building in March of 2019. Once again, our dear plumber friends, Mike and Jann Kenney, came to the rescue and helped repair the old plumbing and put in new plumbing and fixtures.

Because there is no clinic in Jonestown, people who are sick have to drive to Clarksdale to get medical care. That may not seem like a big deal if you have a car. If you don't, it can be very challenging. So, often times people wait until they are very sick and then call an ambulance. Or they wait until they are very sick, making the treatment more complicated and expensive.

If they had a medical clinic in their own town, the delivery of medical care to them would be much better and much easier.

How would we be able to open a clinic in Jonestown? We attempted a variety of ways but kept falling short. Finally, we decided we would simply hire a Nurse Practitioner and get started. But how would we do that?

In June of 2019, Tony West, our nurse practitioner in Haiti, was in the States for a few weeks. While meeting with him one day, I asked him if there was an association for nurse practitioners in Mississippi. He assured me there was. I told him about our plans in the Delta and wondered if someone at the nurse practitioner's association could offer names of people who might be interested in working at our clinic.

In response, Tony told me there was a lady named Karen Bedells who is a nurse practitioner who knows many other nurse practitioners. Tony called her, and she said she would be happy to meet with us. The next week Tony, Rusty Hall, and I met with Karen. She said she worked with a clinic called Rankin Rural that was located just south of Jackson, Mississippi. She thought that clinic might be interested in expanding their services to the Delta. She said they were already approved by the state, had their Medicaid and Medicare numbers, and might be able to turn our clinic in the Delta into a satellite clinic.

We were going to meet the following week with the doctor who is the medical director of the clinic, but he was on a mission trip in another country. As it turns out, this doctor, Michael Albert, is a good friend of Tony West. Wouldn't you know it?!? Finally, several weeks later we met with the medical director as well as the three owners of the clinic. They are very interested in moving forward and opening a clinic in Jonestown. We explained that we were interested in someone who could provide a "clinic in a box." In other words, they could simply set up the clinic with the personnel and equipment necessary, along with the ability to accept Medicaid and Medicare patients. Dr. Albert assured us that Rankin Rural had that ability.

About that time, we also met with Aaron Sisk, the President of Magnolia Health, a Medicaid provider in the state of Mississippi. Their parent company, Centene, generously provided a contribution to help with the clinic renovations in Jonestown. In addition, they want to help in other ways to make the clinic as successful as possible. We have met numerous times with Aaron, and he is very excited about the clinic and wants his company to participate.

Soon, the clinic should be open, and the residents of Jonestown will have access to quality medical care.

EDUCATION

A quality education is one of the keys to a good life. Regardless of where you live, if you cannot read and write and do math and science, then you're most likely going to live a difficult and poverty-filled life. Of course, we can all name that one guy who dropped out of school in the third grade and went on to be a multimillionaire, but he is the rare exception to the rule. For everyone else, a bad education is a gateway to a terrible life. Because this is true, education is a priority for us at BGM.

When we arrived in Jonestown, we were not sure how to get our foot in the door regarding education. Like many of the smaller communities in Coahoma County, Jonestown has its own elementary school. After sixth grade, the children go to a consolidated middle school and high school.

A small way in which we first started to help in the area of education took place at the elementary school. They are the Jonestown Elementary School Warriors. The principal told us that the students can earn Warrior bucks through good behavior and good grades. Several times a year they can take those Warrior bucks to the Warrior store and buy a toy or a game as a reward for their efforts. Unfortunately, they do not have a strong PTO that can write a check for the items that are needed to fill the Warrior store. We asked the principal for a list of items that would be appropriate for the store. She sent the list and most of them can be found at a local Walmart or similar store.

We realized this would be an easy project for Sunday school classes, churches, or similar groups. On one occasion, the children's ministry of First Baptist Church Ridgeland, Mississippi decided to take this on as a project. The parents and children in that ministry brought bags and bags filled with toys and educational games. I loaded the trunk and backseat of my car and took them to Jonestown. When I arrived at the elementary school, a lady helped me take the items to the Warrior store inside the school. She told me she was so grateful because there had been times in the past when the children had worked very hard to earn their Warrior bucks yet when they went to the Warrior store there were very few items. I told her she would never have to worry about that again! Our people would gladly help reward children who had worked hard.

Shortly after we started working in Jonestown, we learned that Sister Teresa and the other nuns were retiring and moving back to the Pacific Northwest. They were looking for someone to continue the work of the Jonestown Family Center. As mentioned earlier, JFC consists of a toddler program for two year olds, a Montessori for three to five year olds, and a fitness center. Initially, they thought Catholic Charities from Jackson, Mississippi was going to take it over. However, that fell through.

One day while talking with Sister Teresa, she asked if we would be interested in acquiring JFC. Rusty Hall and I had been giving this some thought and were glad to hear that Sister Teresa was thinking along the same lines. This was, of course, very important to Sister Teresa because she had spent 30 years of her life investing in this school. She did not want it to go away. Plus, it was very important to the community. We negotiated with the sisters and the local JFC board for many months, and then in 2018 we acquired the school. This acquisition included two buildings, the land on which the buildings sit, one van, one bus, and all the furniture and equipment in the buildings.

Our first full year of operating the school began in the fall of 2018. We've had some changes in leadership at the school, enrollment has increased, and things are going well. Too often in rural Mississippi, children start school, and they are already behind. They don't know basic things like numbers or letters. Then, each year they get further behind and never catch up. Our goal is to have these children ready for first grade when the first day starts. We want them ahead of the game and ready to learn even more. Ultimately, our goal is to expand JFC so that every child in the Jonestown area has a chance at a quality education.

HOUSING

Decent housing is a critical need in Jonestown. Unfortunately, there are numerous houses in which people are living that are in terrible shape. We have learned that a number of families are living in horrible conditions in which they are paying $400 per month to some slumlord who lives out of state. As we considered this, we thought it would be far better for someone to pay that same amount of money for a brand new house while paying a mortgage and building equity.

To this end, we have partnered with an organization from Auburn, Alabama called Third Lens. Brian O'Neil is the director of Third Lens. As stated on their website, Third Lens is a Christ-centered nonprofit organization that, "Engages professionals in the construction and design industries to volunteer on humanitarian projects across the globe." There are only a few full-time employees at Third Lens, but they call on architects and engineers to help with various projects around the world. These professionals volunteer their time as a way to give back to the community. We have been working with Third Lens for over a year to redesign a neighborhood in Jonestown and to design multiple housing options.

Thus far, we have houses ranging in size from 800 sq. ft. to 1400 sq. ft. Brian, from Third Lens, has made many trips from Auburn, Alabama to Jonestown to meet with a community focus group we put together. We told the focus group that we wanted to hear their hopes and dreams for their community. We did not want to tell them what we thought they should have in their community. After all, they are the ones who live there, and it is their community.

After a few meetings, we brought several housing designs to them and asked for their critiques. At first, they did not want to share their thoughts. They are nice people and did not want to appear to be rude. However, we told them to tell us if they liked the plans or didn't like them. We asked them to make suggestions or changes. After a while, they began to share their thoughts, and we were able to make appropriate adjustments to the plans.

We will not be giving houses away in Jonestown. Instead, each homeowner will have his or her own mortgage. We have been working with two financial institutions to make this dream become a reality. Southern Bancorp has agreed to make the construction loans, and Hope Credit Union of Jackson will turn those construction loans into a mortgage.

When we first began researching the possibility of home loans, we met with Phil Eide at Hope Credit Union. I said, "Phil, I have one question. Will you give Miss Suzie Smith from Jonestown a 30 year, fixed rate, low interest loan on $50,000?"

Phil said, "If she qualifies, yes. That's what we do."

I said, "That answers my main question. Let's proceed."

We now have the house designs and the financing lined up. Now potential homeowners must apply for the construction loan. We are close to having the final cost for the various houses we plan to build. Soon we will be building new houses in Jonestown.

EVELYN

One small way we are engaging in economic development is through feeding our teams in local restaurants. Part of the fees that each team pays when they come with BGM on a mission trip is used for lunch and dinner. We want to put money into the local economy. As I thought about this, I believed it would be nice if the restaurants where we took our teams looked nice. So I called a friend of mine, Amy Dear, who lives in Oxford, MS. Amy is one of those get-er-done kind of people. You know the kind. They take on an assignment and ten minutes later they have a color-coded notebook, and the entire process is totally organized.

I said to Amy, "Would you come to Jonestown and meet Evelyn? Listen to her hopes and dreams for her restaurant, and while you are listening, look around to see if there are ways we could help improve the look of the store."

Amy said, "sure."

Evelyn Veasly is a remarkable lady. She was a lieutenant colonel in the Air Force when she retired. She lives in Southaven, MS, just south of Memphis, but she has family members living in Jonestown. Upon her retirement, they asked her to come to Jonestown and open the store. She agreed to do so, invested a lot of her own money, and has been serving the residents of Jonestown for several years now.

The week after my first conversation with Amy she drove to Jonestown. She got out of her car. Then the other three doors of her vehicle opened and six ladies who are get-er-done women like Amy also got out of the car. I thought to myself, "This is going to be good." We walked into Evelyn's store. She cooked us a delicious lunch and then shared with us her dreams for the store. We prayed over Evelyn, and the ladies began making their one hour trip back to Oxford. An hour later, my phone rang. It was Amy. I said, "What's up, Amy."

She said, "We have a plan."

I said, "I thought you would." Ten days later, Amy and twenty-six of her friends showed up and painted and remodeled. When they left, the store looked great!

About that time, I received a call from Lance Reed, the owner of the Chick-fil-A in Oxford. He said, "Stan, I've earned a prize from the Chick-fil-A headquarters in Atlanta. They're going to redo my entire store. I don't need my store to be redone but they're going to do it anyway. All of my chairs and tables and booths are in perfect condition. Would you happen to know of anyone who could use them?"

I said, "I certainly do." And for several years now I have eaten lots of good meals on Chick-fil-A tables in Evelyn's restaurant.

FUTURE

Our goal is to duplicate our efforts in Jonestown all over the Mississippi Delta. God blessed us to duplicate our efforts in Haiti by building a second sustainable community a few years after building our first one. The two communities look different, but the approach is the same. We are simply implementing our SPHERES model of ministry approach in both locations. We learned many valuable lessons in the process of duplicating that first community, but the greatest lesson we learned is that it can be done!

We believe God has blessed us with resources, people, education, knowledge, contacts, and everything necessary to do this work. In fact, sometimes I think God must be saying, "What more can I give you people? I've given you everything you need to make a significant difference in the lives of people in your own state." It seems that the only question is whether we have the will to do it.

Stan Buckley

CHAPTER 13

Growth, Blessings, And The Future

God has blessed BGM more than we ever could have asked or imagined and He has done so in a very short amount of time. In less than eight years, he has allowed us to:

- Build two communities in Haiti
- Open two medical clinics
- Treat tens of thousands of patients
- Deliver over 500 babies
- Open a mini-hospital for starving children
- Build over 150 houses
- Build and operate an orphanage
- Build two church sanctuaries
- Move dozens of families out of tent cities and into new homes
- Hold countless Bible studies and VBS's
- Sponsor over 900 children in local schools
- Build two elementary schools
- Build two secondary schools
- Host thousands and thousands of people on mission trips
- Employ 150 Haitians full-time

- Start our first work in the Mississippi Delta
- Build a 6,000 sq. ft. Hope Center in the Delta
- Open a dental clinic in the Delta
- Open a legal clinic in the Delta
- Operate a school in the Delta
- Create jobs in the Delta
- Host numerous Christian sports camps and VBS's in the Delta
- Host hundreds and hundreds of people on mission trips in the Delta

Throughout the first eight years of our work, God has provided financially in remarkable ways. Once again, the growth we have seen has been very encouraging. In fact, from 2013 to 2018, we have seen an increase of $1.7 million in annual giving.

2013 - $871,920
2014 - $1,244,524
2015 - $1,673,519
2016 - $2,152,415
2017 - $2,325,788
2018 - $2,619,333

On January 2, 2019, I sent an email to the BGM Board of Directors, our missionaries, and employees. I shared the wonderful news about the record breaking end-of-the-year donations we had received. Then I shared with them how I had been thinking about the reasons people give. I don't know the specific reasons for every single person, but I believe there are some general reasons people continue to support our work with their finances. The overarching reason is because of the sovereignty of God and His blessings on our work. He has chosen to bless BGM, and we are very grateful. Under the umbrella of God's blessings, there seems to be three primary reasons people give to BGM.

The first reason is <u>TRUST</u>. No one gives to an organization they don't trust. People give to us because we do what we say we are going to do. We spend the money they give in the way we have promised to spend it. We spend general budget money in ways that are reasonable and effective. Our most recent audit revealed that our administrative costs were 9.5%. That's incredibly low. Also, we refuse to spend funds in ways that are wrong, unethical, illegal, or ineffective. Our donors trust us to use their gifts wisely and in accordance with our stated mission of sharing the love of Jesus Christ through building sustainable communities.

The second reason is the <u>NATURE OF OUR WORK</u>. Much of the work we do is very tangible. You can see it and touch it. Houses are being built. Patients are being treated. Water wells are being dug. Jobs are being created. Beds and benches and tables are being built. Children are being sponsored in schools. Classrooms are being built. School is being held daily and children are learning to read and write. Children are being fed at the schools each day. Churches have been built. Worship services are being held multiple times each week. VBS, women's Bible studies, and Pastor Training sessions are being held throughout the year. The nature of our work is very specific and tangible and not general or abstract.

The third reason people give is <u>RELATIONSHIPS</u>. Most of the people who give have some type of connection with us. They've been on a trip. They know one of our missionaries or our board members or our other donors. They are members of a church where I've been blessed to preach. They have a friend or relative or co-worker who is already involved with us. In Mississippi, this seems especially important. As already stated, Mississippi is not a state, it's a club. Everyone knows everyone, and God has allowed us to capitalize on this reality. Of course, we need to expand our donor base beyond personal relationships because that is such a finite number, but that's what it has been thus far.

The President of our Board of Directors, Buddy Huff, has given the following reasons that people are willing to give: "It is just pure Kingdom work that folks have been able to get involved in, hands-on, very specific vision and intentions. I think people are grateful for that and want to be a part of such. Folks also like to give to something they can see happen, a house for the homeless, a water well for the thirsty, a clinic or a lab for the sick, a church where lost people can worship a living God. That opportunity is provided through BGM, and donors can touch it or see pictures of it or hear testimonies of the experiences. One of our most effective means of spreading the word has been real life testimonies, where experiences are shared and evidence is abundant that lives have REALLY been changed. We have not just talked it, our Lord has blessed and it has happened! I thank my God for every thought of HIS work, not just the successes, but the challenges along the way that have strengthened us all. And a word to our staff, every one of you. You are doing things the right way, with efficiency and with love. Every opportunity is carried out, every challenge is met, every child's sponsor is well-handled, every thank you and acknowledgement timely sent. That makes a big difference with people and makes them want to stay involved. Thank you all!"

FUTURE FUNDING

One way we are funding our work is through the Circle of Hope. The Circle of Hope consists of people who give $100 per month to BGM. Every year, Circle of Hope members receive (1) a beautiful coffee table book depicting our work in Haiti and the Mississippi Delta, (2) a BGM t-shirt, and (3) an invitation to a special dinner with BGM leadership to hear the latest updates and vision for the future.

As I have said many times, as long as BGM is healthy more people will be discipled, more houses will be built, more patients will be treated, more children will be educated, more jobs will be created, more clean water will be made available, and access to healthy food will continue.

Our initial goal was to have 200 people in the Circle of Hope. We started in February of 2019 with just a few people. By July of 2019 we had almost 100 people in the program. Members of the Circle of Hope believe in our work and trust us to spend their gifts wisely and in accordance with our stated mission of sharing the love of Jesus Christ through building sustainable communities.

FUTURE PLANS

I am very excited about the future of BGM. There are countless opportunities to share the love of Christ in Haiti through planting churches, training pastors, expanding medical services, creating clean water systems, sponsoring more children in schools, building more houses, creating more jobs, and providing better access to healthy food.

In the Delta, we are just getting started. I can't wait to move to our next town in the Delta and begin implementing our SPHERES approach. Our plans are to move into as many Delta towns as possible and see an entire region transformed.

ACKNOWLEDEMENTS

I want to thank all the people who have supported But God Ministries over the years through going on a mission trip, giving financially, and sharing words of encouragement. This has been a team effort and the team has many people who have cared and shared so much.

I want to thank Bobby and Dottie Hill for allowing me to write the first part of this book in their guest house in Texas. I want to thank Paul and Barbara Powers for allowing me to write the second part of this book in their cabin in Mississippi. I would never have started or finished this book if I had not gotten away from the routines of work and life to do nothing but write.

I am grateful to Beth Rigney who edited this book and corrected countless comma mistakes.

I want to thank my children – Adam, Neal, and Anna – for their support as we started But God Ministries. Also, they have been to Haiti countless times on mission trips and have fully supported this work.

I must thank my wife, Jewell, for her undying support when we transitioned from my role as a pastor to my role as the founder and leader of But God Ministries. Without her, none of this would be possible.